FORWARD!

THE REVOLUTION IN THE LIVES OF THE FOOTPLATEMEN 1962–1996

C. DAVID WILSON

SUTTON PUBLISHING LIMITED

First published in the United Kingdom in 1996
Sutton Publishing Limited
Phoenix Mill · Far Thrupp · Stroud · Gloucestershire

British Library Cataloguing-in-Publication Data

ISBN 0–7509–1144–1

Typeset in 11/12pt Ehrhardt.
Typesetting and origination by
Sutton Publishing Limited.
Printed in Great Britain by
Butler & Tanner, Frome, Somerset.

Contents

The enginemen were in quite a different class and from the first they showed a particular sense of independence.

(Kingsford, *Victorian Railwaymen*, p. 4)

Acknowledgements

In preparing this book numerous people and organizations have given a great deal of help and information without which it would have been impossible even to begin the story. I should like to record my thanks to all those who have helped, above all to driver Hobson, his wife Muriel and their family – driver Hobson for the time and effort in visiting me and recounting the story of thirty years as a footplateman, and his family for their patience and consideration in putting up with his prolonged absences. My thanks also to my friend and partner Anne Reuss for countless hours enduring the banter of two old railwaymen as they relived their youth.

Intercity East Coast are due a big thank you. Also to Jeff Nichols, Sue Wells and David Mallendar at East Coast Public Relations in York, for the details of the press coverage and their part in providing me with footplate access. To Inspector Neil Gillies, for his company and readiness to answer my endless questions, during my footplate trip with driver Hobson. To driver Jimmy Woolf and the rest of the crews at Gateshead who make the East Coast route tick. I would also like to say thank you to Keith Tomlinson, Driver Training Manager for Regional Railways North East, for giving me an insight into the new training methods and for letting me have a go on the driver training simulator – playing at being an engine driver again was great fun.

Thanks are due to Clive Groome, an ex-Nine Elms driver whose work *The Decline and Fall of the Engine Driver* has been of great help in preparing this book. I should also like to say thank you to George Revill and Tim Strangleman: to George Revill for his permission to use details of his work on footplatemen's identity and to Tim Strangleman for some useful insights on disputes over the boundaries of control of the railwayman's working environment. Thanks are also due to Roxanne Powell for the definitions of the APT and TGV, as scientific and medium-tech solutions respectively, in the question of high-speed railway services.

I would also like to thank Peter Semmens, driver Ron Smith, Colin Marsden and Brian Morrison for their photographs and permission to use the speed and timing details of the record-breaking run. Thanks are also due to Reed Publishing – *Railway Magazine*, Ian Allan Publications, Thomas Nelson and Sons, Leading Edge Publications, David and Charles Ltd, Mechanical Engineering Publications, Frank Cass & Co., Verso, Silver Link Publishing, Manchester University Press, Pitman & Son, G. Allen & Unwin, Locomotive Publishing Co., the *Journal of*

Transport History, Fisher & Unwin and Hugh Evelyn, for permitting the use of quotes from the works listed in the bibliography. Thanks too to Dave Daniels at Elliff Photo Rail for all the efforts with some very old negatives and to Geoff Reiss for computer guru things.

Introduction

The railways have played a unique role in society for close to two centuries, and of all the different occupations that the coming of railways spawned none has caught the public imagination to anything like the degree that the 'engine driver' has. The engine driver controlled a machine that was the wonder of the age – described at the time as 'Promethean', a defier of gods and bringer of fire. The combination of elemental forces, bound and controlled, was and to some extent still is a powerful symbol. The difference today is that the elemental forces being controlled are those of the atom, rather than the fire, air and water of the nineteenth-century steam locomotive.

It is a truism that human beings have a predisposition towards 'being in control'. Those who exercise control, in whatever form, from the hand–eye control of the artist to the manipulative control of a Svengali, have a fascination for those who lack this attribute. The footplateman was the visible representative of an organization with a degree of control which at the time was unsurpassed. For many years the London & North Western Railway, for example, was the largest company in the world; in its control there were thousands of miles of lines, more than 60,000 men and women, vast sums of money and assets; its chairmen were lords, whole towns were in its thrall. The key word in all this is control. Control over vast sums of money, over huge numbers of employees, over great distances, over primordial forces, even over time itself – the railway's role in standardizing time throughout Britain is widely recognized.

In view of the conditions which prevailed at the time the railways were born it is not surprising that they came to occupy the social standing they did. The philosophers of the eighteenth-century Enlightenment had already made significant strides on the steady march of progress towards 'scientific' rationalism; the rise of Utilitarianism and the beginnings of ideas on natural selection were also an important part of the agenda as the railway age was born and began to grow. These doctrines and philosophies have become the cornerstones of the modern world, but at the dawn of the railway age they were in their infancy.

The railways embodied the new ideas of the age, for example they provided the first practical use for the discovery of electricity – the telegraph. Perhaps more importantly, certainly from a railway perspective, the employment of electricity was a means of solving a problem of control and it is the issue and difficulties surrounding control, both social and technical, that were the major obstacles for the new railways. Thus not only did the railways pioneer the first uses of the latest products of scientific thought and experimentation in technology, they also pioneered new forms of social and financial control, without which there was no guarantee that the railway would have been successful – being able to control the vast system that was the railway was an absolute essential if it was to operate safely and prosperously.

Railways helped to push forward much of what we take for granted today. Standardization and time management were both improved by the demands of the expanding railway system in much the same way as it pushed forward improvements in metallurgy, machine tools and engineering techniques – civil, mechanical, electrical and even hydraulic. The railways striving to be bigger, faster and more reliable placed demands on existing technology and encouraged new methods of everything from organization to engineering, finance to steel making; in so doing they created new industrial landscapes, new models of social organization and novel methods of capital raising. For the individual they presented new ways to see the world, created new relations between time and distance and facilitated the growth of a global market in goods and services.

Urban life, commuting, architecture and even the ability to control an empire were influenced or made possible by the success of railway transport. New diets, new life styles, new social institutions, sea-side towns, country spas, mail order, national daily newspapers, regional stock exchanges, even new methods of waging war all owe the railways an important debt in their growth and prosperity, or in the case of the latter in the ability to provision, mobilize or evacuate. The railways were in many ways analogous to the catalyst in a chemical reaction – they could not be seen in the final product, but the product would not have been there without their influence in the process.

Being involved in an expanding industry, one which brought obvious benefits across a diverse range of other businesses and institutions, was almost bound to provide those involved with such an undertaking a degree of standing not enjoyed in other areas of economic and social life. Though he did not play a part in creating this situation, nor yet in the management of the industry bringing it about, the footplateman enjoyed a unique position within this new enterprise. His was the hand on the throttle of the new machine – he was visibly the controller of the new forces, and it was to his charge that the passengers were entrusting their very being.

In their day the railway enginemen were not unlike the astronauts of the early space age: they were pioneers, operators of what was seen by many as a frightening new development, one which could and sometimes did explode with terrifying consequences. As the controllers of this very latest piece of technology their status, in the eyes of their fellows, was a mixture of awe and reverence on the one hand and fear and jealousy on the other, a mixture guaranteed to give them almost cult status. For as long as the railway managed to hold on to its special status, then footplatemen have maintained their status and independence. Until the 1970s, for example, how many 'ace' enginemen were of Afro-Caribbean or Asian ethnic origin?

From the very beginning speed was always an important factor in the railways

– indeed it could be seen as the *raison d'être* of railways. Throughout the one hundred and sixty years or more between the Trials at Rainhill and the new passenger train speed record set in June 1995 there have been a great many speed record attempts, not all of them official. Setting new records – establishing new standards of excellence, as the corporate mission statement might read – is practised in all spheres of human activity: there is an almost universal exhortation to do better, to improve, to refine. What is sometimes forgotten, however, is that the breaking of records involves personal goals and ambitions every bit as much as it embodies corporate excellence or engineering supremacy.

Practically everyone has heard of *Mallard*, but few would know who Sir Nigel Gresley was and fewer still would ever have heard of driver Duddington of Doncaster – *Mallard*'s driver back in July 1938 when she set the world record for steam locomotive traction. In 1995, by contrast, the electric locomotive was virtually indistinguishable from its train and – unlike *Mallard* – lacked any form of charisma; its designer, likewise, was not some knighted chief mechanical engineer. Thus the only real continuity is the driver. Driver Walter Hobson and his co-driver Jimmy Woolf, the new holders of the British Railway passenger train speed record and the focus of this study of the footplateman's life, needed the same degree of fearlessness in running their train as was exhibited by driver Duddington. No amount of technology or management jargon is ever likely to replace the essentially human attributes which are brought to bear in the activity of record breaking.

The purpose of this book is to tease out the threads which weave together the increased levels of railway technology with declining numbers of staff, and driver Hobson's experience of being a mainline fireman in the last days of steam with those as a record-breaking driver in the air-conditioned cab of the class 91 electric locomotive at 154 m.p.h. The varied styles and types of man management, from the near-despotic paternalism of the Victorian age, to the alterations in working practices which were brought into being by the assimilation of Continental and American management techniques, are further strands in the patterns of change which are so much a part of railway life over the last three decades.

There are few, if any, industries with the history and traditions of the railway; footplatemen can trace their ancestry back to the dawn of the industrial revolution. It is almost thirty years since my own footplate career ended and all contact with the working and operation of the national network went with it – the 1990's footplateman and his air-conditioned cab, cruise control and computer-controlled anti-slip devices inhabits a different world from the steam age locomotive footplateman. *Forward!* is the story of this revolution and of the railway's evolution through the social and technological changes of the 60s and 70s, through the 80s reactions and on into the 1990s, hailed by some as the 'new age of railways'. *Forward!* is also driver Hobson's story, bringing together the macrocosm and microcosm of railway operation and management.

The setting of new speed records is one of the more romantic aspects of the engineman's life. The reality, however, is less about careering at full tilt and much more about testing and preparing, checking and re-checking painstaking details. It takes a great deal of meticulous planning to set new records, although on the day it still requires the determination of the engineman to bring it to life. Thus, though there is no lack of romance in numerous aspects of the engineman's life, *Forward!* does not present a romantic view of life on the footplate. It is about the men of the footplate, and especially one man of the footplate, in the form of driver Hobson. It is about their work, the environment in which it is performed, the pleasure and the obstacles, the big picture and the small. *Forward!* is about a body of public transport workers for whom record setting is part of the job specification, which itself has been written and rewritten, a centuries-old tradition, a history linking the birth of the industrial age with the computer generation. What follows is the story of those men and their traditions, the lives they led and still lead and the records they set.

CHAPTER 1

As It Was

A virtual revolution has taken place in the working lives of footplatemen, particularly over the last two decades – indeed, the very title 'footplateman' is now something of an anachronism, as the cabs of the modern traction now in use on the railways cannot be described by any stretch of the imagination as a footplate. In this chapter the focus is on the footplate from its infancy to the advent of 'modernization', the antecedents, if you like, of the modern-day engineman. Its purpose is not to give the definitive history of footplate work, but to highlight the conditions, traditions, practices and culture of the working lives of the footplate crew into which today's enginemen were initiated at the outset of their railway lives. Subsequent chapters will show the extent of the revolution that these men, and latterly women, have experienced.

Black 5, probably 44932, and either a rebuilt Royal Scot or Patriot class stand alongside a brace of English Electric Type 4s. The scene is very reminiscent of the period of change from steam to diesel, though the absence of mountains of clinker and ash is unusual. The site is Upperby shed in Carlisle.

That particular form of employment described by the word footplatemen, as the engine driver and fireman are collectively known, began when the first crude attempts were made to introduce steam traction to the plateways of the collieries and ironworks of early nineteenth-century Britain. The Middleton Railway in Leeds, sanctioned in 1758, began using steam locomotion on a commercial basis in 1812, William Hedley's *Puffing Billy* was in action at Wylam Colliery in 1813 and Stephenson's locomotive *Blucher* followed in 1814, at Killingworth. The use of steam locomotion continued to grow on the plateways, Scotland seeing its first steam traction in 1817. Less than ten years later the Stockton and Darlington Railway was opened, soon followed by the Liverpool and Manchester, Canterbury and Whitstable, Leicester and Swannington, Leeds and Selby and others, creating a growing demand for footplatemen.

Northern England and Tyneside, in particular, was an area with both a well-developed coal and iron industry and a well-developed plateway system. The pit owners of this region began to provide time and money for experimentation to find alternative means of haulage to the horse and the steam-driven winding wheel. The growing demand for coal, the ever-increasing length of the plateway systems themselves and rising costs in the provisioning of the huge numbers of horses being used daily were all important factors which led not only to the development of steam traction, but also to many early footplatemen emanating from this region of northern England.

Another element in the predominance of north-easterners in the early days of railways was George Stephenson, born and bred on the Tyne; Stephenson himself was on *Rocket*'s footplate at Rainhill, but for the purposes of daily operation there were regular paid crews. Stephenson's involvement in the early railway growth was such that he was often consulted on such matters as crewing, and as a result recommended men he knew, or put forward the names of other worthy candidates recommended by those with whom he already had done business: 'The inventor of the first successful steam locomotive had created a "caste", based initially in Northumberland; a "caste" which had its own pieties and systems for handing down its esoteric skills' (Groome, *Decline and Fall*, p. 18).

Footplate life and railway workmen, at least according to some accounts, are a little known and largely unrecorded aspect of the great history of railways, in which the engineering triumphs, the locomotives and the companies which owned them have taken precedence. For example Professor Jack Simmons observes, 'Real difficulties lie in the way of anyone who attempts the task [a history of railwaymen] . . . very few ordinary railwaymen have ever been articulate, able to record their experience and to pass any useful judgement upon it' (Simmons, 'Foreword', p. 16). This all too frequent view that the workman is incapable of making any useful judgement about his working life is often shared by management, and many a disaster, both physical and financial, has resulted from management's failure to involve the rank and file employee, especially in regard to the work's operational aspects and the equipment used to perfom it. This feature is as much a part of working life today as it was in the last century.

There is another and perhaps even more important stumbling block when trying to write about the lives of footplatemen. Over the years, from the last century to today, a great number of over-romantic accounts – books, pamphlets and magazine articles – have been written about footplate life, and footplatemen themselves have contributed to this. What is perhaps most revealing about all these works is their very existence: after all there are few if any works entitled *How I Became a Capstan Lathe Operator*, or *Ace Dustbinman*. There is no other area of manual labour which has had the attention or coverage that has been enjoyed by the footplateman. In words, photographs and logs the footplateman's life has been examined, scrutinized, dissected and envied in a manner not shared by other working–class occupations. Unfortunately this has had a number of less than beneficial side effects; for the footplatemen there has been a suppression of their wages, for the historian there are the distortions created by the romanticizing of the true nature of footplate work.

In October 1981 Walters [Alan Walters, economic adviser to Prime Minister Thatcher] told the Adam Smith Institute in London: 'I would love to see many railway lines in private hands. They may do wonders. It would be very nice to get out of railways. *The real wages you need to pay railway drivers are very low. People would almost pay you to drive a railway train.*'

(Bagwell, *End of the Line*, p. 2, my italics)

Through the window, a driver's eye view of an approaching freight working, in charge of one of the Hymek Type 3s, which were peculiar to the Western Region. The location is the Down main between Maidenhead and Twyford.

Walters' view is not uncommon and there is no doubt that, out there in what is frequently referred to as the 'real' world, a small army of would-be enginemen are all eagerly awaiting the call. However, even this group might baulk when confronted with having to do the job on a daily basis, especially on discovering that eight hours round and round the Kingston loop, or its many equivalents, week in and week out, at every hour God sends, is in fact not in the least romantic. Indeed, it can really only be described as soul-destroying: 'The drivers of multiple unit electric trains live a more solitary life; one turn at Waterloo is known as the "face at the window turn" because the only company the driver has in 8 hours is his own reflection in the cab windscreen' (Groome, *Decline and Fall*, p. 55).

There is undoubtedly an element of romance in the railway, as poems like the 'Night Mail' or those of the railway poet William McGonagall attest. However, workings such as the Night Mail or the famous named trains like the 'Flying Scotsman' or the 'Caledonian' represent only a tiny fraction of railway work – in the steam era these workings accounted for less than 10 per cent of traffic, and if shed turns are included they represent less than 5 per cent of all footplate duties. By concentrating on these high-profile duties the picture of real footplate work is very much distorted. Over time these distortions have come to be believed.

The issue of the footplatemen's alleged inability to formulate coherent ideas about their work is partially refuted in their attempts to protect themselves from the less romantic aspects of their work and the conditions under which it is carried out. The *Locomotive Journal*, which is the house magazine of the Associated Society of Locomotive Engineers and Firemen (ASLEF), the footplatemen's trade union, opens its very first edition with quotes from Thomas Carlyle, Thomas More and Plato. That the originators of the footplatemen's magazine were erudite enough to know of these writers and felt sufficiently at home with them to be able to present them to their membership, with every expectation that they would be read and understood, goes at least some way to refuting the comments of Professor Simmons.

Some railway managers, however, maintained the view that footplatemen were an illiterate bunch, well into the twentieth century:

> As late as 1919, Mr Harry Earl was told that the locomotive superintendent for the Great Western Railway at Worcester, when congratulating prospective drivers, advised them to 'keep good control of the firemen', because the majority of locomotive-men were recruited from the land and were of low mentality and little education: one of the major sources of this enmity [between townsmen and countrymen] was the countryman's docility, [all too often taken to be stupidity] the very quality which made him attractive to his employer.
>
> (McKenna, *Railway Workers*, p. 29)

In the 1840s the directors of the London & North Western Railway appeared to take a rather different view of the importance of the degree of intelligence and education of their employees:

Not all railway work involved dashing about on express passenger workings: the humble tank engine was a veritable maid of all work, especially on the old GWR. No. 9635, a member of the 57xx class, stands by the water column waiting instructions.

The Directors consider the proper education of young persons a matter of such vital importance that they cannot but look with distrust at the man whose negligence condemns a child to ignorance. . . . The Directors hope for special attention to the extension and improvement of education among their servants; they trust that the London & North Western Railway will be distinguished by the intelligence and morality of those engaged on it and be a pattern for other great establishments.

(Kingsford, 'Labour Relations', p. 70)

The pious words of the London & North Western Railway directors were backed up with concrete action; by 1859 there were seven company schools and financial support was given to some non-company schools in areas where there were concentrations of railway employees. The other major railway companies were less altruistic: the Great Western, the Great Northern, the South Eastern and

Eastern Counties Railways each had one school and the Manchester, Sheffield and Lincoln had two. As to the rest, it would seem education was of less importance.

Although the directors of the London & North Western Railway appeared to be acting altruistically, it is possible to argue that, as the efficient operation of a railway system was predicated upon the adherence to an ever-growing body of operational rules and regulations, a literate and numerate workforce was a functional imperative. Seen in this light such altruism simply becomes 'enlightened self interest'. The actions of railway employers in other aspects of their business confirms the view that the provision of educated workers was merely an act of self interest.

For whatever reason, there is no getting away from the fact that, with one or two notable exceptions, biographic accounts of the life of railwaymen are in short supply. Biographies of railway managers are almost as deficient, although in the latter case there is no shortage of evidence for managers' activity. The activity of railway management, in relation to the railway employee, has, more often than not, been one of 'master and servant'. This is the view of the directors of the London, Brighton & South Coast Railway in 1852:

> The directors are in principle opposed to combination [unionization] of any description for the purpose of interfering with the natural course of trade. They think that masters and men should be left in every establishment to settle their own terms, arrange their own differences without foreign interference or dictation.
>
> (Bagwell, *Railwaymen*, p. 19)

Of course what constituted 'the natural course of trade' was not a matter for discussion, and most definitely not with the 'men'. The differences in power, control and authority between the railway management and their employees was obviously a crucial factor in determining settlements between them.

Employment practices in the early years of the railways are characterized by a form of paternalism, draconian levels of punishment for what seem to be very minor indiscretions, inhumanly long hours of work and a degree of militarization of the workplace, both in terms of the way in which the daily duties were performed and also the language used to describe them.

> From the 1830s to the present [1970], railway labour-control techniques and terminology have reflected many aspects of military life. The essential difference between railway work and the armed forces appeared when the railway workers realized that by carrying out their orders to the letter they would reduce the train services to a shambles. This working to rule turns the concept of obligation upside down.
>
> (McKenna, *Railway Workers*, p. 30)

Kingsford is no less emphatic when he concludes:

relations between labour and companies were notable for their peacefulness. Disputes and labour organisations were significant for their comparative rarity. This may be attributed to those conditions of work which encouraged either satisfaction or loyalty to the companies, to the nature of railway work, and to methods of labour control. Chief among these were security of employment, prospects of advancement, strict discipline, mobility, the divisions between grades, and the policy of 'divide and rule'.

(Kingsford, 'Labour Relations', p. 81)

The divide and rule philosophy has been an important element in labour control policy from the very earliest days of mass labour, and is the main tactic employed to break up labour disputes. The continued use of this practice says much for its efficacy: '"Divide and rule" was a routine method as well as one used with special force during disputes; the practice of using one grade as a check on the other was general' (Kingsford, *Victorian Railwaymen*, p. 77).

The different emphasis in Kingsford's and McKenna's conclusions is due to

An unidentified King, possibly No. 6019 King Henry V, *runs into Paddington with a 'holiday' excursion working in 1963.*

the fact that the former is only dealing with the period prior to the advent of the railway trade unions, whilst the latter covers the period in which trade unions were active. Despite the quasi-paternalistic tone of some areas of employer/employee relations, conditions were so harsh that collectivization was the only way in which the employee could hope to improve his situation. Holidays, for example, which we now take for granted, were unheard of for many railwaymen even in the twentieth century.

> Holidays were unknown to a great many Locomotivemen in Britain. On a number of systems they worked day in day out, year after year, and very seldom did they have even Sunday free. In 1904 the actual position was that holidays with pay were not granted on the G.C., G.W., L&N.W., the N.E, or on Scottish or Irish Railways.
>
> (McKillop, *Lighted Flame*, p. 81)

In addition to the less than pleasant employment practices there were many operational difficulties encountered on the early railway system; inevitably there were those which resulted in considerable loss of life and liberty. Frequently the footplate crews involved in accidents (those who survived, that is) were put on trial for manslaughter and gaoled as a result. The arrest and trial of footplatemen, following fatal accidents, was common practice until the 1880s when the footplatemen formed their own trade union, ASLEF. That fewer footplatemen were then gaoled was brought about mainly by the union providing legal representation, rather than by industrial action. Subservience was far more rife than militancy, which was hardly surprising given the lack of welfare provision on the one hand and the fate of strikers' leaders on the other – six months' hard labour on the treadmill was a common sentence for those adjudged to have been active in promoting the stoppage, a sentence which would have condemned their families to the workhouse. Many of the railway companies also kept and circulated to other companies a list of known 'agitators', who would be denied employment as a result. This practice was partially responsible for the emigration to America of a large number of former footplatemen, who subsequently became drivers on the American railroads.

The first relatively effective railwayman's union was the Associated Society of Railway Servants, which began to act on behalf of its membership in 1871. However, the ASRS lacked militancy, organization and, as far as footplate crews were concerned, did not understand their position. It did little more than present paper requests which management largely ignored. The aims of the ASRS were 'To promote a good and fair understanding between employers and employed; to prevent strikes; to protect members against injustice . . .' (Bagwell, *Railwaymen*, p. 28). The protection of members against injustice is not only a reference to the practice of putting railwaymen on trial following serious accidents, it is equally concerned with the arbitrary application of fines and other punishments, particularly those imposed by the lower grades of railway management. Similarly, the aim to prevent strikes cannot be described as trade union militancy. The ASRS was largely ignored by the railway management, however, who ruled pretty much like feudal lords: 'had the trade union wanted to inculcate a spirit of hatred towards railway officialdom nothing that they could have done would have instilled it more firmly than the actions of the railway officials themselves' (McKillop, *Lighted Flame*, p. 45).

The early footplatemen had to be a hardy breed, for the engines they drove had little or no protection from the elements – there was an anecdote common among railwaymen in the 1950s and 60s, which was often used when conversation turned to things past: 'Eeh them wer' t' days when thi 'ad wooden engines 'n' iron men.' Many early locomotives did have a great deal of wood in their construction, and without cabs and weather shields the crews must indeed have been iron men, particularly so when one considers the number of hours spent on these exposed footplates. Despite the vicissitudes of footplate work there were no shortages of men willing to take the work on, and it has to be said that the work was not without its compensations, of which there will be further discussion later.

Long hours and heavy-handed management are only part of the footplateman's lot: the early railwayman had to contend with unreliable equipment, poor or non-existant signalling, lack of protection from the elements, roughly laid permanent-way, bad riding engines and, as a result, the ever-present possibility of serious mishap. Many of these issues took years to resolve, indeed some of them are still present during driver Hobson's career. McKillop is clear where much of the

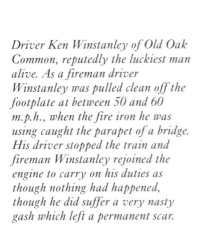

Driver Ken Winstanley of Old Oak Common, reputedly the luckiest man alive. As a fireman driver Winstanley was pulled clean off the footplate at between 50 and 60 m.p.h., when the fire iron he was using caught the parapet of a bridge. His driver stopped the train and fireman Winstanley rejoined the engine to carry on his duties as though nothing had happened, though he did suffer a very nasty gash which left a permanent scar.

blame lies: 'It is a terrible indictment of early railway management that it fought every attempt made on behalf of even the most elementary safety measures' (McKillop, *Lighted Flame*, p. 9). As a footplateman and trade unionist, McKillop might stand accused of bias. However, Colonel Yolland, one of Her Majesty's Railway Inspectors, and the *Daily Telegraph* appear to agree with him:

> with the exception of a very few railway companies that recognised the necessity and acted upon it, it may be truly stated that the principal railway companies throughout the Kingdom have resisted the efforts of the Board of Trade to cause them to do what is right, which the latter had no legal power to enforce.'
>
> (quoted in Nock, *Railway Engineers*, p. 39)

Here is what the *Daily Telegraph* says about the pioneer footplatemen in the 1860s:

> The reason why there are not 10 accidents where we have 1 is the praiseworthy pluck and perseverance of thousands of poor fellows, who, with a noble sense of enormous trust imposed upon them, have not permitted either abuse, tyranny or oppression to impoverish their integrity or honesty.
>
> (McKillop, *Lighted Flame*, p. 11)

The excessive number of hours on duty was one major source of accidents: 'In respect of hours, however, there is ample evidence to show that the railwaymen were often intolerably overworked and that excessive hours of labour were a contributory cause of the very high accident rate on the railways' (Bagwell, 'Early Attempts', p. 95). The *Railway Year Book* gives some indication of the dangerous nature of railway work in figures for deaths and injuries to railwaymen. In the period 1896 to 1913, 120 railwaymen were killed and 51,208 were injured; in the years before 1896 matters were even worse, with deaths running at nearly ten per week and injuries at more than fifty. Part of the decline in the mortality rate is undoubtedly due to improvements in medical science, which kept men alive who in former times would have perished from their injuries. Some idea of the excessive hours and management's attitude towards them can be gauged from these comments made by an anonymous guard:

> A guard at Leeds told me, that having been at work eighteen hours, he was requested to take a train to London. The tired and sleepy man went to the superintendent and respectfully asked him how many hours he was expected to work? 'That's our business' was the official answer, 'you've got twenty-four hours in a day, like every other man, and they are all ours if we want you to work them.'
>
> (Kenny, *Men and Rails*, p. 139)

Initially the growing railway network created such a demand for footplatemen that the railway's trade paper, the *Railway Times*, could comment, 'at first the demand so far exceeded the supply that companies were glad to secure servants of this class on any term, and a driver was no sooner dismissed from one line for misconduct than he found ready employment on another' (Bagwell, *Railwaymen*, p. 19). This situation was not to last long, however:

> Most men, once they had been fortunate enough to secure such employment, were careful not to jeopardize their positions by such reckless indiscretions as joining a trade union and taking part in strikes. . . . There can be little doubt that the scales were heavily weighted against any trade-union activity on the railways during the first forty years of their rapid expansion. In view of the odds against those men who did attempt to organize their fellows it appears all the more courageous.
>
> (Bagwell, *Railwaymen*, pp. 20, 28)

It is worth reflecting on the fact that from the very infancy of railways there has been such a fascination with engines and with driving them that it crossed class and occupational boundaries. Noblemen and clergymen, doctors, lawyers and bank clerks all had a yen to be engine drivers. One consequence of this attitude has been to undermine the footplateman's ability to improve his working conditions and pay:

> A railway strike to be effective must achieve its objective in the first few days. Every schoolboy at some stage of his school life longs to be an engine driver. Many retain this longing on reaching adulthood and only have an opportunity to fulfil their ambition on the occasion of a railway strike.
>
> (Bagwell, *Railwaymen*, p. 396)

During the General Strike of 1926 this is precisely what happened. In strikes in the nineteenth century blackleg labour, with no skills, no knowledge of the rules or any other aspect of railway work, were hired to break strikes, often being helped in their task by junior management or non-striking workers in other grades, such as guards, shunters and foremen.

Such have been the changes in the fortunes of the railways that it is now possible to be both doctor and engine driver – on one of Britain's private railways. This change has come about partially at the expense of the 'professional' engine driver; indeed, this is perhaps one of the most fundamental of all the changes that have taken place in the public perception of the engine driver. Today's engine driver sits in very much the same air-conditioned environment that the passenger rides in, and at journey's end he turns a key and locks a door – no different, in many respects, to putting the car in the garage. Herein lies one of the paradoxes of the railwayman's life: as the value and sophistication of the technology under his control has risen, his status and pay have deteriorated.

> The oral evidence of the ex-steam drivers, many of whom started on the railway in the 1940's, can now be examined. The majority, 85 per cent, have experienced a decline in job satisfaction since the ending of steam traction. An

A1 No. 60158 Aberdonian *exits York, bound for the North. None of these handsome engines survived the modernization programme – though progress is currently being made in building a replica, to be numbered 60163, the next number in the series allocated to this class. The engine is to be named* Tornado, *not an entirely appropriate choice for a class which was originally named after birds, pre-Grouping railway companies and the locomotive designers who worked for them or the characters from the novels of Sir Walter Scott.*

old saying is proved to be true by the fact that 75 per cent of the drivers gave as the reason for starting on the job, 'the fulfilment of a boyhood ambition'. Interestingly, the men that came on to the footplate merely as a matter of chance – 'it was just a job' – have experienced the greatest loss of job satisfaction.

(Groome, *Decline and Fall*, p. 38)

For a great many years, from the beginning of the nineteenth century until the later decades of the twentieth, the air of 'schoolboy romance' surrounded the job of engine driver. Timothy Hackworth, whose locomotive *Sans Pareil* was a competitor at the Rainhill Trials, sent his son to Russia, ostensibly to show the

Russians how to reconstruct the kit of parts that was the locomotive he had supplied them with. However, Hackworth junior was not only expected to reconstitute the kit of parts, he was pressed into service teaching the Tsar himself how to drive the engine. The Tsar's interest went beyond the supply of the locomotive: he had also apparently been to Britain trainspotting: 'Young Hackworth relates that he was introduced to the Tsar Nicholas who told him of a visit paid to England in 1816, before his accession to the throne, when he had witnessed with great pleasure the running of Blenkinsop's engines on the colliery line from Middleton to Leeds' (Young, *Hackworth*, p. 276).

Public reaction to, and perception of, the work of the engine driver is strangely ambivalent. Despite the romantic attractions of the job that have already been alluded to, passengers will tip a waiter for bringing their order to the table and walk past and ignore the engine driver who has just brought them 300 miles in safety. There have always been people who believed that little or no skill was needed to operate a locomotive and haul a train: one such person was the so-called 'Railway King' George Hudson. In an effort to reduce costs and turn a profit Hudson forced his footplatemen to take a wage cut (macho management is not some new feature of the 1990s: it was a Victorian value too). Coupled with increased hours of working, the end result of Hudson's actions was a strike by the men. Hudson immediately dismissed the strikers and began to hire blackleg labour, but the lack of skill amongst the scab labour led to numerous accidents and damage to the rolling stock and locomotives. Hudson's draconian measures were overturned at a hastily convened board meeting, and most of the strikers were reinstated.

In fact, footplatemen are not a particularly strike-prone section of the labour force – the first national rail strike by footplatemen was not until 1911, a hundred years after the trade of footplateman began – but what the Hudson incident did show was that if they did strike, running train services with unskilled staff was a risky and potentially disastrous way to manage a railway company.

The problems most commonly associated with the early railway undertakings were those facing almost all new and untried technologies: for example the reliability, or not, of the new technological artefact and the materials used in its construction; safe operating methods; and the level of understanding and knowledge of the correct means to achieve a safe operating standard. When one remembers that the early railways had loose-coupled trains, hand-operated brakes on the engine, or more often only on the engine's tender, and the guard's van was the only means to stop the train once it was in motion, with only time-interval signalling to co-ordinate their movements, then it becomes clear just how easily serious accidents would have occurred if unskilled men had been asked to operate the network.

Probably one of the most outstanding features of footplate life, which was nurtured from the start and is still in force today, is the degree of company loyalty and inter-company rivalry. Rivalry between companies, between depots and even between crews in a link were, and are still, very much a part of footplate work. In most cases the rivalry was good humoured and no doubt provided a degree of esprit de corps – an esprit which in view of the dangers and hardships of footplate life would have helped the men not only to perform their daily routine but on occasion to act with great selflessness and even outright heroism.

Although 'self help, self-sacrifice and a sense of morality were important elements in the preservation of railway loyalty' (McKenna, *Railway Workers*, p. 44), the most essential aspect of footplate work, at least until the advent of diesel and electric traction, was teamwork. Driver and fireman were a team; their opponents were the locomotive, the coal and the gradients, not forgetting the load behind the tender. On the diesel or electric locomotive the degree of power and performance is predetermined by the horsepower of the diesel engine or traction motor. With the steam locomotive the relationship between it and the horsepower it could deliver was mediated by the perfomance of the crew – as a result power and performance were much more subjective phenomena. Unlike the diesel or electric locomotive driver, the steam locomotive crew have a symbiotic relationship with the engine, and only by the skilled application of their teamwork would the locomotive actually deliver its potential power output.

Old and new: the guard with his paraffin hand lamp and the shunter with his pole are from another age when compared with the image being created for the diesels. The location is Old Oak Down sidings and the engine is one of the Birmingham Railway Carriage and Wagon Company/Sulzer Type 3s allocated to the Southern Region. This particular locomotive has been fitted for push-pull working.

The relationship between the crew and the locomotive is an important issue for a variety of reasons. The locomotive represents a considerable investment to the capitalist, one which by its very nature is open to abuse, through ignorance or design, by those employed to use it. Unlike most capital equipment the steam locomotive and to a lesser degree its modern counterpart were not under the direct surveillance of either the capitalist or his paid overseer or manager, a situation which placed a great deal of responsibility on the driver, who was held to be the responsible party on the footplate – the fireman being under his jurisdiction.

In the railway's infancy the most common method of alleviating this particular problem was the system whereby only one or two crews shared an engine – thus introducing some element of ownership and thereby some degree of respect for the machine by those crews involved. This practice was widespread and persisted for well in excess of a hundred years, though this does not mean that it was a perfect solution. It certainly encouraged a sense of pride and gave status to the footplate crew. The relationship between management, men, pride in the job and respect for the equipment is an important issue in railway work and, as will be seen in subsequent chapters, these abstract concepts can and do have important consequences.

> Thus was created a new form of industrial anthropology, a tribalistic grouping of men based on an elaborate division of labour, a hierarchy of groups and a ritualistic adherence to territory, myth, symbolism and insignia unknown outside the specified boundaries.
>
> From the earliest days, the railway companies sought a new type of loyalist, nothing less than a prototype, a (sic) 'organization man'. They achieved an outstanding success, and for more than a century the workers demonstrated a loyalty to newly founded tradition and working methods unique in British industrial history. In the railway industry, the Protestant ethic, militarism and nineteenth-century paternalism met and were cemented into specific loyalties which retained their potency long after amalgamations of 1923, or the advent of public ownership in 1948.
>
> (McKenna, *Railway Workers*, p. 41)

The issue of company loyalty is an important and complex one; some of the reasons for its existence have already been referred to. One which has not yet been mentioned is the company-sponsored friendly society, more than fifty of which had been formed by 1870. Other forms of financial ties and inducements were utilized, but not all of them had the long run outlook of the friendly society. Many companies used devices such as monthly, quarterly or, in some instances, biannual bonuses for saving coke, coal or oil to encourage economy of operation and respectful use of property as well as to help retain the workforce.

Before discussing the changes to railway work brought about by the activities of the trade unions, there needs to be some consideration of the actual working practices and conditions on the footplate. The early locomotives were crude in the extreme, lacking even the most rudimentary forms of equipment:

There were no brakes on either engine or tender, and the only way of controlling the train down the banks was to put the engine out of gear, or for the fireman to drop off the engine and let down as many waggon brakes as was thought necessary. . . . There was neither gauge glass nor whistle, a bell serving as a note of warning, nor were there any hand lamps. . . . At night a large pan of fire was affixed to the front of the tender [which was propelled] and to the last waggon . . . and it was the duty of the fireman to keep both alight.

(Young, *Hackworth*, p. 295)

The early locomotives lacked other amenities: the injector did not come into common use until after 1866, the continuous vacuum brake only became widespread after the Railways Act of 1889 and many locomotives lacked anything resembling a weather-proof cab, even in the twentieth century. There were numerous locomotive types which did not have any seats for the driver, never mind the fireman, and tender first workings not only left the crew facing the elements, but covered in coal dust as it blew off the tender – you cannot keep the coal properly slaked when running tender first, as the water blows back in your face rather than soaking the coal.

Keeping steam locomotives at work for long periods leads to clinker building up in the firebox. As this would stop air getting to the firebed, thus reducing the engine's steaming capabilities, the fireman would have to try and break it up and improve the air supply if the engine was in motion; if the locomotive was at rest he would dig the clinker from the bars and then shovel it out of the firebox using a long metal shovel, commonly referred to as a 'paddle'. At the end of every turn of duty the firebox would be cleaned, and men would enter the firebox to carry out any maintainence, or routine tasks such as sweeping the brick arch, replacing burnt firebars, caulking firebox seams, or re-beading weeping tubes. It was not unknown for these tasks to be done with small amounts of fire still in the firebox, so as to speed the turnaround time and get the locomotive back in traffic. These practices were still an essential part of railway work until regular steam workings ceased in 1968.

The operation of a steam locomotive is dirty, arduous, back-breaking work interspersed with periods of tranquillity. Every day on the footplate is a challenge, making steam, keeping time, battling gradients and elements. Young's description of the life of the footplatemen of the Stockton and Darlington Railway gives some idea of the prevailing conditions at the dawn of footplate life:

Their lives were rough and dangerous, were exposed to all weathers and never sure when they started out in the morning when they would get safely back again. In comparison with the locomotivemen of today [1923] their lot was hard and the life thankless but they did not lack excitement and variety, and there was an absence of restriction and a certain independence of action which was prized by them.

There were always plenty of applicants for vacant positions, and they worked not on fixed wages but by contract, and made good money.

(Young, *Hackworth*, p. 293)

Contract working was not uncommon in the early years of railway development. Drivers would have to pay for their own coal or coke and oil plus the fireman out of their contracts, which were often based on the number of loads hauled, a practice which was open to abuse and risk taking. The most common form of risk taking seems to have been speeding: 'and John Farden in the same company's service, [Stockton & Darlington] an early victim of the lust for speed, was fined 5 shillings on January 15th 1830 "for furiously driving whilst coming down the run"' (Bagwell, *Railwaymen*, p. 26; 5 shillings (25 pence) was roughly a day's pay at the time the fine was levied).

There are two forms of speeding: 'official' speeding such as the record made by driver Hobson and his fellow footplateman driver Jimmy Woolf, and unofficial speeding which is, as driver Farden discovered to his cost, a punishable offence, for any driver caught exceeding the line speed limits could, in the most extreme case, be dismissed and even imprisoned if the speeding was considered to be reckless and a danger to the travelling public. There is a third aspect to the speed

Driver Farden would have been working on something like this when he was fined five shillings for 'speeding down the run'. This is the Locomotion *replica on show at the Shildon Cavalcade held to celebrate 150 years of the Stockton and Darlington Railway.*

issue, that of running to time. If a train should be delayed for any reason, it was the practice for drivers to try to make good any losses by running harder between stops – though of course they were not actively encouraged by management to break the speed limits. And it is worth noting that until the last decades of steam traction steam locomotives were not fitted with speedometers – thus the actual speed at any given moment depended on the driver's good judgement alone.

The setting of speed records, which was actually part of the design brief for competitors in the Rainhill Trials, has been a feature of railway operations from that time. The two most important forms of speed record have always been the 'highest all-out burst' and the 'start to stop average' over a particular journey or part thereof, such as the record for the journey between London and Aberdeen set during the 1895 'Railway Races to the North' or, in the case of the top speed dash, *Mallard*'s 126 m.p.h. on the descent of Stoke Bank in 1938. In setting these records the steam locomotive footplate crews were being asked to produce the utmost in performance from their locomotive, which inevitably required them to perform to the same record breaking level, particularly the fireman, upon whose ability to raise steam aplenty the whole effort depended – though the poor fireboy seldom rates even a mention in the often copious literature surrounding these record-breaking events.

The railway companies used speed as a major selling point in many of their attempts to drum up new trade or poach trade from their rivals by offering quicker, more comfortable and convenient services, not only to passengers but also to those customers consigning freight and parcel traffic to the railways. The early contracts with the Post Office saw either demanding schedules, for example those set by the management of the London & North Western Railway to run the Holyhead Mails, or out and out racing, as was the case between the Great Western and the London & South Western in competing for the Plymouth or 'Ocean Mails'. Spectacular, sensational – no matter what epithets are applied to record attempts and high-speed running, the fact remains that in the steam era these events imposed considerable extra strain and work on the footplate crews, and as the locomotives grew in power and weight the efforts demanded of the fireman grew proportionately. As one footplate wag commented, 'They only made one mistake when they built the big engine: they should have arranged with providence to build a big fireman as well' (McKillop, *Lighted Flame*, p. 155). Writing on the same topic, McKenna says,

> Although the engines doubled in size [1900–1955] hand shovelling was still the means of feeding the furnace, and these engines [the *Gresley, Bulleid, Peppercorn, Stanier* and *Riddles* Pacifics and the like] were probably the ultimate in what a man could do with a shovel. Only men who worked on these engines in full flight can appreciate the awesome power of steam locomotion. . . . A mainline fireman had to keep in tip-top physical condition. He needed hard muscles, a supple back and no fear of hard work, for on a long run there could be no escape from the toil and strain. . . . The firing of steam boilers owed little to theory and much to practice. Firing skills were achieved on the footplate in traffic.
>
> (McKenna, *Railway Workers*, pp. 141, 145)

No. 60007 Sir Nigel Gresley *heads the White Rose past Copley Hill shed en route for the capital in the last days of steam on the Leeds–London service. (photograph © R.W. Smith)*

The final sentence in the extract above makes a very important point about footplate work, that the skills were learned on the job in service. In some areas this apprenticeship could last for many years: men were still firemen at forty, after fifteen or more years' service in that role. However, as the twentieth century progressed, in some areas firemen became drivers on reaching the age of twenty-three and thus never spent more than seven years at most as firemen. Driver Hobson's railway career illustrates this point, and in chapter 2 these wide disparities will be given a more comprehensive explanation.

Not all footplate work is about long-distance running. In general terms the important and long-distance workings are the prerogative of the top one or two links at each depot, and so would only involve the top 20 per cent of crews. In the lower links the crews would spend their days shunting, empty stock working, on trip goods or on the even more arduous 'shed turns' where the crews would prepare engines for duty or dispose of them after they had completed their allotted day's work. This type of work was just as physically demanding as working the mainline express service, but without any of the honour and glory associated with the crack express. For every 'top shed' with many express passenger turns to cover there are half a dozen smaller depots whose workings might well be nothing more exciting than the operation of some small branch line – a job which many might describe as a sinecure, though not those who actually do the work, such as this ex-Bournemouth footplateman working push-pull trains:

> but when pushing the fireman's duties were not only to fire the engine, but also to keep an eye on the Westinghouse pump, operate the controls of the locomotive, regulate his boiler steam and water level, listen for 'bells' from the driver and watch the brake when stopping. . . . I always considered the push and pull link was the hardest link at Bournemouth and because of no night work or overtime the worst paid. You spend all day chasing about on a Drummond tank, climbing all over it to trim coal and take water many times a day, as well as burning a bunker full of coal and knocking some clinker out of the fire; you knew you had been at work. I was not sorry to get out of that link.
>
> (*Railway Magazine*, 138, no. 1094, 1992, pp. 33, 77)

Although the work of each footplate crew had many common elements it was enormously varied; footplate experience depended very much on which depot they were based at. Whatever the depot, however, the rivalries remained: these could be expressed in various ways from good-natured banter to applying personalizing touches to the locomotives, or, if the rivalry extended beyond their own company, hijacking complete locomotives and even harrassing passengers.

The rivalries that existed between the major nineteenth-century railway companies were carried over into the amalgamations of 1923 when 120 individual railway companies became just four, the London Midland & Scottish (commonly referred to as the 'Midland'), the London & North Eastern (which was shortened to 'North Eastern'), the Southern and the Great Western. These four companies suffered their own internal problems as a result of pre-existing rivalries, and their formation generated new traditions and new rivalries.

The 'Grouping' was followed by the General Strike of 1926 and then by the Depression, both of which greatly influenced railway life and work. Many of the concessions gained after 1911 and again at the end of World War I, such as the guaranteed eight-hour day, twelve hours' rest between duty and improved pay and holiday conditions, all came under threat between 1923 and 1935.

> Over the decade from 1923 to 1933 the full effects of the amalgamations of the old companies into four main groups were being felt more and more by railway staff.
>
> The apathetic attitude of railwaymen towards their trade union in the early 1930s was brought about by the stagnation of rates of pay and conditions in the fifteen years since 1919 and the infamous 2½ per cent plus reduction of wages forced upon the trade unions. This 2½ per cent levy on the wages of railwaymen to assist the companies was an outstanding example of the fallacy that sacrifices by employees can solve the economic problems of employers in big industries.
>
> (McKenna, *Railway Workers*, p. 129)

Adam's 0-4-4T No. 36 Carisbrooke. *This photograph, taken at Ryde MPD in 1963, shows an engineman oiling the Westinghouse pump, as referred to in driver Evans' letter commenting on the life of the footplate crew in the Bournemouth MPD Push and Pull link. Everywhere you look there are piles of smokebox ash and clinker; to the left of the engine is the primitive coal stage. Behind No. 36, No. 14* Fishbourne *waits her turn. Strangely, No. 14 and No. 36 were first and last of the Adams 02s transferred to the Isle of Wight; the majority were transferred after the Grouping.*

The amalgamation also created a large number of redundancies and men often had to move miles from their homes to stay in employment. The figures from the *Railway Year Book* tell their own story. In 1921 there were 38,665 drivers, 37,097 firemen and 21,302 engine cleaners (the lowest footplate grade). In March 1923 the numbers were 36,708 drivers (almost 2,000 down), firemen were almost unchanged at 36,698, but the cleaning staff had shrunk by almost 9,000 to 12,765. The figures for 1962 when driver Hobson started as an engine cleaner were 35,910 drivers (almost unchanged), 22,692 firemen (which represents a reduction of one third) and a mere 2,590 engine cleaners.

The position of Cleaners and young Firemen on the railways was deplorable. As junior members of the staff, they were first to become redundant, and

Old rivals side by side. Ex-Southern Railway U class No. 31635 stands alongside the Great Western Railway main line at Reading.

thousands of them were forced to abandon their homes, not once but on many occasions, and to lead an almost nomadic existence, moving from depot to depot to keep themselves in a job.

It must not be surmised, either, that because they were junior in the grade they were juvenile in years. This was no trek of the unencumbered lad. Since in thousands of cases these unfortunate men had served the railways from 5 to 10 years, and were married men with families, one does not require a vivid imagination to picture the lives they were forced to lead.

(McKillop, *Lighted Flame*, p. 195)

On top of the threat of redundancy, the poor pay and the arduous nature of the work, an even greater threat faced many a footplateman as his working life came to an end:

In almost every European railway concern the employees were safeguarded by retiral pensions. In every case the widows and orphans were given an allowance if death intervened. It seems fantastically paradoxical that Britain, a world-leading nation, should have employees on many railway systems giving anything up to fifty years of service, and at the close of their careers being flung pensionless on the scrap heap.

True, certain of the old companies, notably the Great Western, had a pension scheme, but there was no national and uniform system; and far from improving the position in this respect, the new group railways were out to demand a worsening of it.

(McKillop, *Lighted Flame*, p. 167)

(In the extract above, McKillop is describing the conditions prevailing in 1925. The pensions on the European railways, to which he refers, varied between 60 and 80 per cent of the final wage, with an average of 75 per cent. The employee's contribution varied between 2½ per cent and 6 per cent of his wage.)

The image projected by the railway companies following the Grouping, and particularly in the 1930s during the Depression, was one of improvement, growth and opulence. It was the era of the streamliners, of Art Deco cocktail bars on Southern Railway commuter trains, of *Beaver*-tailed observation cars, of the *Gresley* and *Stanier* Pacifics and the quest for speed – the era in which the world speed record for steam locomotive traction was set. A very different picture is revealed when one investigates the relationship between the management and their employees. This, for example, from McKillop, who was himself a footplateman during this period:

It has been stated that the trade union movement took an unfair advantage of the war situation [i.e. World War I]. I have not seen it asked whether the profit-making chaffering of world commerce, which lies at the bottom of all wars, considers it quite fair to ask the common man to sacrifice his life to secure these profits, and at the same time to deny him a reasonable share in them.

(McKillop, *Lighted Flame*, p. 109)

The Races to the North of 1895, which involved the five companies then operating the East and West Coast routes to Aberdeen – the London & North Western and Caledonian on the West Coast, the Great Northern, the North Eastern and the North British on the East Coast – are mirrored in the streamlining and speed record attempts which took place during the middle years of the 1930s. Similarly, all-out speed record attempts were made in the 1960s following the electrification of the West Coast route as far as Liverpool and Manchester; there were similar attempts following the introduction of the Deltics and High Speed Trains on the East Coast route. The record-breaking attempts that followed nationalization and the 'modernization' of the railway network, however, no longer relied on the steam raising abilities of the fireman.

The men who were on the footplate, as firemen, during the 1930s and 40s were the engine drivers of the 1950s and 60s. These men had been firemen to drivers whose own careers had begun when the Races to the North were being run in 1895. When driver Hobson began his own railway service in 1962 he did so alongside men who had been schooled by those who had worked the services in Victoria's reign and had themselves worked the system during those speed record days of the 1930s and through the difficulties and hardships of World War II. The rivalries and traditions which had originated in the nineteenth century were thus transmitted to men who still run today's railway.

The intense competition for trade which had manifested itself as the Races to the North at the end of the nineteenth century can be seen as a precursor of the rivalry which still exists between the East Coast and West Coast train operating companies. The improvements in traction and engineering on the two routes have both resulted in the setting of new speed records; the attendant publicity has been used to promote that route at the expense of the other. The current East Coast advertising hording, for example, launched less than three months after the establishment of the new speed record, proclaims the East Coast 'Britain's fastest railway'.

After the cessation of hostilities in 1945 a Labour government was elected and the 'Big Four', as the grouping companies were known, became nationalized as British Railways. The four large groups were replaced by the regions. The Great Western and the Southern remained more or less as they were, the LMS, which became the Midland region, lost its Scottish territory, as did the LNER which was divided into the Eastern and North Eastern regions (it later also gained some territory from the Midland). The Scottish railways became the Scottish region. Despite being all one railway the rivalries still remained, both at the footplate level and, more importantly, in the boardrooms and drawing offices. Though these struggles are not the main concern of this narrative, it is essential to have some understanding of the events following nationalization to fully appreciate the difficulties and dilemmas facing footplatemen as the century has progressed.

At the head of the British Transport Commission was Sir Cyril Hurcomb, later Lord Hurcomb. (One of the Riddles Britannia class Pacifics was to be named after him.) The British Transport Commission was given wide ranging powers: 'exclusive monopoly over railway transport, over the transport of goods by road over distances exceeding forty miles and over transport by inland waterway, and provides for eventual control over road passenger services' (Hurcomb, *Organisation*, p. 3). Interestingly, in view of the current debate over railway privatization, Hurcomb took a very different line to that currently being peddled:

> Physical development is a field in which nationalisation has advantages. . . . Again a nationalised undertaking is likely to find it easier than any private commercial enterprise to take a long view, to time its investment, to go ahead with physical development at a time when unemployment is increasing and labour is available, and thus to assist in maintaining full employment.
>
> (Hurcomb, *Organisation*, p. 23)

Nationalization was seen as beneficial by a great many rank and file railwaymen, and following the official hand-over many of them chose to celebrate:

On the Sunday following the change over, the National Union of Railwaymen

'Riddles' Austerity', the epitome of utility. In the 1950s and '60s no goods yard scene was complete without its 'Dub Dee'. This work-stained example is No. 90694. After nationalization it was one of the first of the Austerities to enter BR service, being allocated to Pontypool Road depot on the Western Region. The engine in the photograph appears to be carrying a 56F Low Moor shed plate; the location is Low Moor.

held mass meetings in many large railway centres. More than 2,000 railwaymen attended the London meeting in a West End theatre . . . Meetings were of different types. Apart from the large meeting in the London Coliseum, at Belle Vue circus in Manchester the New Year was celebrated by the arrival in the ring of the Railway Queen, drawn by a miniature railway locomotive. A Grand 'Gala Dance' was arranged by Paddington No. 3 branch: Peterborough and Darlington held 'socials and dances', Stourbridge No. 1 branch a smoking concert. Other celebrations took place at Hull, Stratford, Pontypridd, Newport (Mon), Birmingham, Newcastle, Swansea and Cardiff. The latter was marked by a speech from Mr. L.J. Callaghan, then Parliamentary Secretary to the Ministry of Transport, in which he argued that 'we ought to have an annual Railway Day to celebrate nationalisation'.

(Bonavia, *British Rail*, p. 20)

(Mr Callaghan eventually became a Labour prime minister in the 1970s, though he never did instigate an annual 'Railway Day'.)

The nationalization of the railway companies meant that for the first time in a century and a quarter conditions of service were set on a national basis. Though this may have removed some of the possible causes of grievance, even rivalry, it certainly did not eliminate the latter. One of the first events undertaken by the supremos in the drawing office – the 1948 Locomotive Exchanges – gave ample opportunity for footplatemen to play out these rivalries to the full. The problem was that the railways were looking at the wrong rivals and asking the wrong questions. Though these were essentially management issues the choices that were made and the subsequent results all had a direct bearing on the working lives of the footplatemen. Bonavia, once a member of the railway's management team, sums up the situation with regard to the Locomotive Exchanges:

> while this was obviously going to provide enormous interest for railway buffs and rich material for railway photographers, it did not seem relevant to the prime question which nearly all major railways in the world were asking themselves – what was to be the future role of steam, diesel and electric traction in the post war world?
>
> (Bonavia, *British Rail*, p. 41)

The Locomotive Exchanges were not the only aspect of the new policy of the Railway Executive which Bonavia singled out for criticism. Equally important are his remarks concerning the introduction of the Standard classes of locomotives and the lack of foresight exhibited by those charged with creating the new transport blueprint: 'it can be argued that the pre-occupation with designing standard steam locomotives was a disaster, it was irrelevant to the needs of the day, and was an exercise in nostalgia, which wasted valuable time and created many difficulties for the Executive's successors' (Bonavia, *British Rail*, p. 46).

The creation of British Railways was flawed from the start. The two bodies, the British Transport Commission and the Railway Executive, respectively responsible for the implementation of a transport strategy and the operation of the railway, were acting at cross purposes at best and deliberately thwarting each other's intentions at worst. One surefire way to bring a business into difficulties is to have a divided management team, unsure of their course of action, fighting their own internecine wars, lacking realistic business plans and presiding over a deteriorating asset, for which too much had been paid. This was the situation on the railways as they faced a severe assault from two of the most influential boom markets of post-war Britain – road haulage and the motor car.

On the rail network itself, early signposts to the way progress would be presented as the railway entered the second half of the twentieth century were the restoration of the non-stop running between Kings Cross and Edinburgh, and gradual increases in line speeds as the ravages of the war were slowly made good. Something else which began to develop at this point was the perceived value of promotion through the manipulation of images, a process which has led to a multiplicity of changes of logo and livery. The practice of designer relaunches and corporate logos was in fact one of the only growth areas as the railway sought to re-invent itself, to make itself more attractive in an era of rising ambition and growing consumerism based on almost full employment

When the steam-driven goods engines had all gone from the old GWR, the Hymek Type 3 took over many of the dwindling numbers of mixed-freight workings. This photograph shows an unidentified member of the class with a through load working in the mid-1960s.

and the resultant increase in affluence across a wide cross-section of the working population.

In the immediate post-war era, 'science was to deliver a bright new future': the century (or more)-old steam-driven railway could not fulfil this dream, and so it was off with the old and on with the new. The diesel and electric locomotive were to be the railway of the future, clean, efficient, needing no fireman – or so the story goes. In 1954, thirty years after Europe and North America had begun their process of dieselization and electrification, diesel multiple units began to make their presence felt. There had been some experimentation with the railbus, rail car and diesel locomotive prior to 1954: the Great Western, for example, introduced diesel rail cars in 1934, and thirty-seven were transferred into BR stock in 1948 along with three from the LMS, although forty twenty-year-old rail cars plus the blueprints for a diesel locomotive and a handful of diesel shunters were hardly the basis for a timetable of modern, attractive and fashionable trains.

Nationalization was a political issue and the railways of Britain have suffered numerous tribulations at the hands of those with political rather than railway agendas. The failure to implement a coherent transport strategy following the end

The scene may look like the Blitz, but it is actually Leeds City Station in the process of being rebuilt. Wearing the 17B shedplate of Burton-on-Trent, Jubilee No. 45620 North Borneo *is waiting departure of its train before running light to Holbeck MPD.*

of World War II and the current strength of the anti-motorway lobby is perhaps the most eloquent testimony to the failure of the British Transport Commission. Interestingly, just as there was an important military presence in the management and control of the early railway network so too was there an important military element in the new management machinery of the nationalized railway – the decision to entrust senior military personnel with responsibility for running a commercial undertaking of the size and diversity of the railway, and in the commercial climate it was coming to inhabit, may have been a classic example of the wrong people in the wrong place at the wrong time. Bonavia concedes that the 'intentions were clearly good', but goes on: 'what (with hindsight) now seems to have been lacking was a realistic appraisal of long-term traffic prospects and the future strength of road competition' (Bonavia, *British Rail*, p. 41).

Some are rather more scathing in their condemnation:

The post-war history of the railways falls conveniently into three phases. The first period covers the years up to 1962 when they were under the care of the British Transport Commission. This was probably the most disastrous period, a time when many opportunities were lost . . . It suffered from a lack of good managerial talent and this resulted in weak and tentative policies.

(Aldcroft, British Transport, pp. 127, 142)

Despite the spread of dieselization and electrification in mainland Europe and North America, British Railways began its life by building more steam locomotives

'Standard Arthur' No. 73086 The Green Knight *rolls onto shed at Nine Elms. Two tranches of this class of mixed traffic engines received names and were allocated to the Southern Region. These were numbers 73080 to 73089 and 73110 to 73119. These free running and free steaming engines were capable of prodigious feats of haulage, and were often entrusted with working the heavily laden boat trains from Southampton Ocean Liner Terminal to Waterloo. Sister engine to 73086, No. 73082* Camelot *has been preserved and restored to working order at the Bluebell Railway.*

– the British Railways Standard class locomotives. These consisted of a whole range of locomotives intended for all types of workings from suburban passenger to heavy freight, which were designed and built in the workshops of the former railway companies, in the main by the same design teams who had produced the A4s, the Duchesses and Bulleid Pacifics. Though the decisions to proceed in this way were to some extent dictated by circumstance and political necessity, there was more than a hint of the old rivalries and traditions, not to mention idiosyncrasy, in some of the chief mechanical engineers' decisions, one of which was a determination to be the last of the great steam locomotive designers.

Among the other changes that took place after World War II, particularly important were those in the sphere of social life and leisure activity. The growing affluence generated in the post-war boom provided new opportunities, one of which was an expansion of literature concerned with and popularizing the railway. Typical of the genre was *Railways the World Over* by G.F. Allen, who died while this book was being prepared. The *Guardian*'s obituary notices commented,

> In the years that followed [his appointment as editor of *Trains Illustrated* and later *Modern Railways*] he developed a new approach to railway journalism, focusing on business, in contrast to the traditional enthusiast magazines, with their emphasis on train performance, tractive effort, and operations.
>
> It gave GFA a unique status within the industry. For the first time, managers could read informed articles on their business and, through the magazine, promote their own ideas. At the same time, these reports also appealed to the more serious enthusiast. Soon the readership exceeded 60,000.
>
> (Ford, Obituary, p. 11)

The growth in the number of books and other printed works (the magazine *Trains Illustrated* went from a monthly circulation of under 20,000 to one of over 65,000 between 1950 and 1960) popularizing and eulogizing the steam locomotive and the men who worked them, also served to perpetuate that romantic image of footplate life in the minds not only of a great many schoolboys, but more importantly amongst the footplatemen themselves. 'Much of the status of the engineman was the result of "reflected glory"' (Groome, *Decline and Fall*, p. 17).

In a roundabout way the decline in the importance, to the national economy, of railway and railway manufacturing led to an increase in attention on the footplateman – especially the steam engine driver. Increasing numbers of enthusiasts rode behind the leading enginemen on the crack trains, the enthusiast magazines carried logs of the timings – who had done what speeds with which trains, hauling how many tons. The footplatemen were photographed, recorded in their work, revered and respected for the performances they produced. When the steam finally ran out, much of this glory went with it. However, even when driver Hobson's railway career commenced in 1962, 'performances' were still being put on, and platform ends were still crowded with boys in grey flannel – 'Can we get on the footplate mister?'

Throughout the 1950s the average schoolboy railway enthusiast could still imagine a rosy future as an engine driver but, as we have seen, the reality was very

The engine is Manningham's last surviving 'Derby 3', and it has been 'bulled up' by (passed cleaner) Hobson for a rather special turn. This was the 'Worth Valley Special', a trip up the Worth Valley branch, a line driver Hobson had worked as a fireman. Shortly after this excursion the line closed, only to be re-opened in 1968 as the Keighley & Worth Valley Railway. The engine No. 43586 was less fortunate and within months of the rail tour was on its way to scrap.

different. The BTC had been reorganized and the road haulage aspect of its remit was removed in 1953, only months into a new Conservative administration. This led to a huge increase in road traffic. In 1955, for the first time, road haulage accounted for more freight carried than the railways; by the time steam finished in 1968 the railway's share of the freight market was down to 20 per cent. On the passenger front things were scarcely better: 'By 1970 the railways accounted for only 8.8 per cent of total passenger movements as against nearly one quarter in 1950' (Aldcroft, *British Transport*, p. 111).

At the end of the 1950s the footplateman's life was still much the same as it had always been. The railway they worked over was the same one the Victorians built, the steam locomotive still provided the backbone of the motive power and apart from increases in size they remained little changed from their Victorian predecessors. Conditions of service were marginally improved, but fifty- to sixty-hour weeks were not uncommon, there was still no comprehensive pension scheme for footplate grades, there was no formal training programme, the operation was labour intensive and the labour was of a heavy manual variety. They continued to adhere to the principals of public service, job first, craft solidarity and a high level of trade union membership.

Personal social relations were, to a large extent, with other footplate crews; many areas had staff association clubs and most depots had a nearby public house in which the crews met and socialized. These features have tended to produce close-knit communities based on shared experience and mutual understanding of the hardships and difficulties of the footplate life. How far this has changed is the subject of the following chapters.

CHAPTER 2

There at the End

Driver Hobson entered the footplate 'caste' as an engine cleaner at Manningham Motive Power Depot in Bradford on 29 January 1962; 'modernization' had been under way for six years, steam locomotives were rapidly disappearing from the more important mainline duties and diesel multiple units were making inroads into branch-line workings. In the West Riding the DMUs, as they were usually referred to, had been at work since 1954. Despite the changes taking place at the technological and increasingly on the presentational level, the drivers for whom young cleaner Hobson was firing were men who had begun their footplate lives in the so called 'Golden Age', the era of racing between the *Stanier* and *Gresley* Pacifics in the 1930s; they had also experienced the travails of war. For many of these men worse was to come, with all the vagaries and alterations of various modernization proposals which have become an almost permanent feature of the railway landscape – arguably only the major amalgamations of the nineteenth century and the Grouping of 1923 come anywhere close to rivalling the changes wrought since nationalization.

In a 1985 interview, Alan Wilton of Nine Elms, an ex-steam driver who had learned his trade from men whose own careers had started before World War I, expresses a view commonly held by those men who started work on the railways around the time of nationalization.

> You felt a sense of achievement on the steam, that is if you *did* pass for driving, that they had accepted you into a standard. And you felt a sense of needing to uphold that – you felt more pressure on you, I *certainly* did, I felt that I can't let the side down because I know all the good blokes that have gone before me, y'know, blokes I fired to – I thought blimey! If I really don't pull myself together here, I'll let myself down and also the tradition of the job down. With freight trains I was always so wary – you've got to bloody well watch what you're doing. You don't feel that now, as [the other chap] said, the blokes joining [today] they feel that it's only a game, in no sense do they feel the tradition because they don't *see* any tradition.
>
> (quoted in Groome, *Decline and Fall*, p. 41)

Thirty years earlier, in conversation with the author Ransome Wallis, driver Harris of Old Oak shed remarked, 'Money is not the only consideration in life – more important to me is the dignity of the position which I have achieved'

Cardiff Canton-based 'Grange' No. 6813 Eastbury Grange *carrying a through freight headcode passes Reading, c. 1964. None of this class survived into preservation.*

(quoted in Wallis, *Footplate*, p. 9). Driver Harris' view was not uncommon and many footplatemen have held posts such as justice of the peace, councillor and mayor; the public service and public duty ethos was common. Indeed, it was an attitude that was fostered amongst the men: 'Railway workers were perceived – and were encouraged to perceive themselves – to be not only employees of individual companies but also servants of the public' (Revill, *Trained for Life*, p. 65). Revill then invests these perceptions with the role of status provider:

As the railway industry was perceived as fundamental to the efficient functioning and increasing strength of the nation in terms of economic and social integration, so the railway worker was a servant of the state. To serve the railway was to serve the nation, and to sacrifice normal life to the requirements of the railway system's obligations to provide total spatial and temporal coverage was to make sacrifices to the good of the nation as a whole. On these foundations rested much of the status of railway workers in society in terms of railway work's connotations of respectability, duty and service.

(Revill, *Trained for Life*, p. 71)

Thus the men on the footplate in the 1950s – and these were the men who were training the young driver Hobson – had been initiated into the footplate tribe and instructed by men for whom public duty and 'job first' came naturally.

Being keen to become an engineman, driver Hobson was eager to learn the job and its traditions, an attitude which has not only supported him through more than thirty years as a footplateman, but is in its own way a part of the tradition to which driver Wilton refers, which driver Harris exemplifies and into which the

Lamps are being changed and a last minute chat is underway as a remarkably clean Hall class 4–6–0 No. 6918 Sandon Hall, *piloting an unidentified Castle, prepares to depart Bristol Temple Meads.*

young driver Hobson was being initiated in the early months of 1962. Undoubtedly there is an element in each succeeding generation that the newcomers are 'not as good as the old breed', but it must be said that some of the conditions which bred the practices which became 'tradition' have disappeared too. Lodging – the practice of working to some distant point from the home depot and then stopping at a railway lodging house, often purpose-built, before returning to the home depot on the next turn of duty – ceased with the termination of steam services in 1968. Only those rogues with a girl in every town mourned the passing of this tradition.

> When I was at Old Oak there was still lodging at Plymouth and at Gloucester. It wasn't so bad if you had a good mate, but at Manningham when I was there we had lodge jobs to Derby and the old Midland lodge was like a barracks – all little cubicles with camp beds, there was a scrap yard clattering and banging out the back and the partitions was so thin you couldn't sleep for the sound of the other blokes snoring and what have you – it was like something out of *Oliver Twist*.
>
> I know this may seem hard to credit, but I had Mike Thamm, our finance director, in the cab a few days ago [November 1995] and he said to me, What did I think about a return to lodging, nearly thirty years after it was stopped. I asked him if he was being serious – as if anyone would want lodging to return.
>
> (driver Hobson, 1995)

Lodging was hardly the sort of practice to endear itself to young footplatemen, especially those beginning a railway career at the start of the 'swinging sixties', but, as that legendary footplateman Bert Hooker points out, it had to be dealt with 'You had to be self disciplined to the extent of overriding domestic issues. It was bred in me that the job came first. We were the largest body of unsupervised men in the country' (quoted in Groome, *Decline and Fall*, p. 41). The tradition of self-supervision among British footplatemen was not duplicated elsewhere; indeed, it was considered far too easy-going by many other railway systems which exercised, or at least attempted to exercise, strict control over the way the driver performed his duties.

> This of course [freedom of action in the control of the locomotive] has long been a characteristic of British locomotive practice, and one that surprises foreign railwaymen, the latitude allowed to drivers in the way they handle their engines, contrasting strongly with the strict control exercised over, for instance, French drivers.
>
> (Bonavia, *British Rail*, p. 47)

Wallis discusses other aspects of the nature of public duty:

> Railway work is not unlike my own work in the practice of medicine, for each exists for the purposes of service to the community. In both, to be competent, you must be keen, and more than keen on your work. You must be prepared to

give much service for which you will never see money and, often, not even gratitude. You must accept, as your reward, the knowledge and satisfaction of a job well done. You must be able to deal with all sorts of emergencies with resource and energy, and not grumble when duty calls you out to work turns you never expected, at any hour, day or night. Such men must remain individualists of the highest order. . . . While uniformity over the whole country may be desirable on paper, these men have been brought up in one great tradition, but with many diverse customs and habits, many of which are very sound in the districts where they are worked. Surely every effort should be made by Unions and Managers to preserve and not to destroy such individualism.

(Wallis, *Footplate*, p. 11)

It is, perhaps, worth remembering that Wallis was writing in 1953. Another of the arguments he was espousing was that enginemen should continue the practice of one or two crews having, or more correctly sharing, their own engine, as had been the case for more than a century on a great many of the nation's leading railways. When driver Hobson started his railway service it would have been almost impossible to operate the one/two crews per engine policy because of the changes in the various types of motive power and the new diagramming arrangements for the remaining locomotive fleet.

A decade later Wallis' remarks are echoed in the writings of Norman McKillop, the legendary Haymarket driver, author, historian and trade unionist:

An ace engineman on the railway is not unlike the best type in the medical profession. They never really leave their student days behind them. They are constantly learning, diagnosing, finding out what the symptoms indicate. The one deals with living tissue the other with thews and muscles of steel and iron – actually, between the two there isn't such a great dividing line.

(McKillop, *Ace Enginemen*, p. 12)

There were much more than ancient practices and long-held traditions for the young driver Hobson to learn, and drudges such as lodging to contend with. The actual working environment was such that it was hard to escape from the notion that you were being inducted into some ancient and mystical society: the smoke-filled cathedrals referred to as the 'shed', men dressed in the often bizarre forms of clothing peculiar to their arcane duties, boilersmiths and brick arch men furtive behind their masks and goggles, often with woolly hats or berets pulled down over their ears (anything to keep out the dust), fitters in blue overalls carrying tallow lamps and huge Whitworth spanners, washout men with their wellies and waterproof leather cowls, like some unknown and ungodly order of monk. 'In that time it was like turning the clock back, there was no difference to me with anybody starting in the early 1900s. The shed was no different to when it was built, only a modern wooden building had been added for the diesel multiple units' (driver Hobson, 1995).

The depot at Manningham was still the original Midland Railway

Impassive and impressive, Stanier Pacific No. 46239 City of Chester *stands in the dappled light of the roundhouse interior at Willesden MPD alongside an unidentified Sulzer Type 2 in the early '60s.*

construction. The high-ceilinged mess room with its coal fire and 'Oldham' gas geyser was practically Dickensian – a far cry from the projected image of a 'modern railway'. The antiquated mess room was only one of the reminders of the railway's Victorian ancestry; another was the brass pay check discs, which had to be presented to collect wages which were paid over in a small, tin cylinder with only half a lid. Protective clothing such as overalls, overcoats, even cap badges were doled out according to the number of firing turns completed; Dayglo vests were unheard of. There were no showers, not even proper washing facilities – most steam footplate crews washed up in a bucket on the footplate before leaving the engine: hardly the right environment or circumstances in which to bring about a revolution in railway working.

Helliwell was the clerk, so rigid, an old 'Derby' man [the term used for men whose careers began with the Midland Railway or one who strongly applied and upheld the traditions associated with that company]; the situation these people were in was they accounted for every penny, the purse strings of the depot.

(driver Hobson, 1995)

If conditions for the staff were poor, the situation regarding the operation of the shed was even worse. Coaling the engines was carried out by crane using 7 cwt tubs. Driver Hobson describes the scene beautifully: 'When a "Black 5" or "5X" came down [on to the coaling stage] or when one of the Britannias with the big tenders came down from Carlisle they used to empty every tub in sight then everyone would be working like crazies to fill them up again' (driver Hobson, 1995).

The state of Manningham depot in 1962 was not unique: many depots still hand-coaled the engines, utilizing either the tub and crane method, as at Manningham, or a 'coal stage'. The coal stage (a brick and wood structure elevated to the height of the tender top) would be alongside one of the shed roads. On one side would be loaded 16 ton coal wagons and on the other small tubs which could be run out and tipped into chutes which emptied into the engine tender or bunker as it stood alongside the raised coaling stage. The tubs were hand loaded from standard coal/mineral wagons by gangs of labourers. The crudity of the actual working situation was in stark contrast to the images which the railway publicity and management were attempting to create.

Footplate work is a tough and demanding job at the best of times, made harder by the lack of investment in the right equipment. The case for a stuctured improvement to the railway and the means by which it was operated was overdue when nationalization was introduced. However, the conflicts and personality cults which so emasculated the effectiveness of the Railway Executive and the British Transport Commission had the effect on the ground of denying resources where they were needed and squandering vast sums in areas where any realistic opportunity for a return on the investment was doomed.

The footplatemen who were doing the job on a daily basis were all too well aware of the yawning gap between rhetoric and reality, amazed that such sums of money could be frittered away while leaving the more pressing difficulties untouched. 'When I was at Old Oak it was just daft: people squatted fire irons, tools, brushes and buckets, you had to come in an hour early to get your engine ready, just so you had time to find everything you had to take with you' (driver Hobson, 1995).

Driver Hobson had been extremely fortunate to be given a start as a cleaner at Manningham. Only months before his appointment a number of junior firemen and passed cleaners had been transferred from Manningham to Heaton – just the same sorts of movements as those forced upon this grade during the immediate post-Grouping period back in the 1920s. The period of 'modernization' between 1956 and 1968, as far as staff were concerned, was not unlike that which prevailed at the Grouping, the difference being that in the 1950s and 60s the movements of men and the redundancies were the result of technological changes. Some idea of the scale of change and the rapidity with which it took place can be gauged from the dramatic differences in staff numbers between 1960 and 1969. In 1960 the

A1 No. 60130 Kestrel *catches the sunlight as she stands alongside the coal stage at Copley Hill MPD. Copley Hill depot was, at the time, responsible for all the main line workings from Leeds over the former LNER routes to the south, and yet despite the volume of traffic coaling was still by hand from the coal stage. (photograph © R.W. Smith)*

railways employed 520,000 men and women, but by 1969 this was down to 296,000 and in 1972 the figure was 196,635 (figures from Bonavia, *British Rail*). With such huge numbers of redundancies taking place it is perhaps all the more remarkable that driver Hobson managed to hang on to his post, for as Bonavia points out, 'The most acute problems were the surplus of footplate staff arising from the change of motive power' (Bonavia, *British Rail*, p. 152).

In addition to the changes taking place in technology and in the size and scale of railway operations there was also an element of social change which was not present in the upheavals of the 1920s, though there were indications even then that the overbearing, militaristic and paternalistic management style of the Victorian railway magnates, following the Grouping of 1923, was being challenged:

The General Secretary [of the Railway Clerks Association] appealed for more consultation between management and staff, arguing that in the past any sense

Bristol based 'Crompton' stands alongside Manningham MPD with the evening 'Bristol Goods', 1963.

of community of interest between the two sides of the industry was destroyed by the feeling that the staff were paid to do as they were told and were not expected to think. These days have passed but joint consultation is even now not a reality. It is often conceded in principle but withheld in spirit.

(Bonavia, *British Rail*, p. 21)

Unlike so many of his compatriots in earlier times, driver Hobson did not spend long as a cleaner – only a matter of weeks. This meant that some classroom training was necessary to enable him to take the necessary exam to become a 'passed' cleaner. The training consisted of visiting the Mutual Improvement Class and a week of instruction from a couple of footplate inspectors. The Mutual Improvement Class, or MIC as it was more commonly known, was run by the men themselves and was designed to help cleaners learn the rudiments and to give firemen the information they needed to allow them to pass the strict exam to become drivers. The MIC also organized other events such as visits to foreign railways and courses of instruction on new forms of traction; it also had – indeed still has – social as well as quasi-training functions.

> They were two good lads – Chris was the union rep and ran the MIC with another driver, Brian Fields. The secretary was a chap called Dennis Sarabank, who has since died. They weren't full drivers at the time; they were old hand passed firemen and they would be in their late thirties. They ran the class – they got it all instilled into us, they really went to town on us.
>
> (driver Hobson, 1995)

Writing of his own experience of becoming an engine driver, Norman McKillop describes the MIC room, which was usually provided by the company, and what the functions of the Mutual Improvement Class were. The key word in the name was 'Mutual': self help by agreement.

> The walls are covered with diagrams of different parts of the engine, braking apparatus, lubricators and injectors, while here and there is a comic picture – poking fun at the users of this much-used room. For there is hardly a day passes but an argument is brought within the MIC room walls. . . .
>   The main function of the locomotive MIC, however, is to encourage drivers, firemen, and mechanics to learn everything possible about their job by mutual interchange of practical knowledge and experience and, of course, in doing so regular classes are held to tutor cleaners and firemen by talks on various subjects, generally from a driver or mechanic.
>
> (McKillop, *Engine Driver*, p. 11)

The learning of the craft of footplateman was generally 'in service', but, as was the case in driver Hobson's early career, there were exceptions. However, classroom learning was only a very small part of the process of becoming a competent fireman and then driver, though there were to be dramatic changes to the training of footplatemen as the steam locomotive was phased out and new methods of working were introduced. Chapter 3 will discuss these changes in greater detail, particularly as the new training methods were such a complete departure from the 'self help' 'in your own time' methods adopted by the steam driven railway companies.

> The practice of locomotive driving is a field teeming with facts and incidents, cause and effect leading up by natural and consistent steps towards perfection through long winter nights in wind and rain, in lightning and thunder, at all times surrounded by hidden dangers, and ending at times in a dreadful, sudden death. A man may have the best of locomotive knowledge, and still, if he is unaware how and where others have met with accidents he will be assaulted by surprises, and his progress will be but slow . . .
>
> (Reynolds, *Engine Driver's Friend*, chapter 1)

The learning process for a trainee fireman could only be taken so far in a classroom environment, as the many different firing techniques could only be fully taught and understood in service. Here again the traditions of the Victorian railwaymen were being brought into question. When driver Hobson started working on the railway:

> I was thrown in at the deep end, really. I didn't start with a pilot job, shunting and shed work or anything, it was a one o'clock in the morning job, tender first to Stourton yard with a 'Derby 4' and work the coal to the Bradford Valley power station – a heavy train for a 'Derby 4', twenty or twenty-five 16 tonners fully laden with power station coal, like black sand.

> (driver Hobson, 1995)

Initially, when driver Hobson started at Manningham, as in many other depots the mix of duties consisted of steam turns with occasional diesel workings beginning to make their presence felt. At the end of 1962 there were approximately nine hundred mainline diesel locomotives in service – almost one third of the total number in service in 1968 when steam working ceased. The 350

Wreathed in steam, Stanier Pacific No. 46250 City of Lichfield *stands under the Cenotaph coaling tower at Willesden MPD. At least this coaling plant is mechanized, although the coal lying around everywhere is par for the course as the steam age ended.*

or class 08 shunters had come into service, taking over yard pilot duties and displacing the 'Jinty' and other classes of 0–6–0 shunting engines; more importantly, from a fooplate perspective, they were taking away the turns on which the young passed cleaner learned the firing techniques which he would put into practice as he progressed in his railway service. However, as we have seen from the example of driver Hobson, the arrival of dieselization meant that men, often very young men (driver Hobson was passed for firing at sixteen), were being put to work on turns demanding a high degree of effort and knowledge to accomplish their work successfully – this inevitably put additional strain on the drivers who were, after all, responsible for the train, its safety and its punctual arrival. In the case of driver Hobson these difficulties were mitigated by his enthusiasm for the work, but not all young footplatemen were as motivated as he was.

Within months of passing out for firing duties driver Hobson was working over the famous Settle to Carlisle route with both the 'Clan' class Pacifics and their bigger sisters the 'Britannias' on stopping trains to Carlisle. He was also sent off

This photograph of rebuilt Royal Scot No. 46109 Royal Engineer *was taken on one of driver Hobson's first firing turns, a trip over the Settle–Carlisle route. The scene is Carlisle Citadel station: the porters' barrows in the background appear to indicate a healthy parcel trade!*

'on loan' to Holbeck depot in nearby Leeds where there were trips over the same route with another of the Riddles designed engines, the 2–10–0 '9F's. The young passed cleaner, who became driver Hobson, was learning his trade in service alright, and over one of the hardest roads in the country. This is hardly the gradual introduction, the slow build up from shunting duties to station pilot, to trip goods to branch or stopping passenger train which had in the past taken anything from eight to fifteen years to undergo – the whole process of acquiring footplate skills was now being by-passed through technological change. What had been years of practice was now being reduced to months. In the words of one of the former members of the British Railways management team, 'Recruitment and training was another field in which the railways were woefully weak. . . . Training is the counterpart to recruitment: it is no use recruiting scientifically if the recruit is not thereafter properly inducted into his work and equipped to perform it' (Bonavia, *British Rail*, p. 89).

Bonavia did not have footplate crew specifically in mind when making these remarks, which have a much wider application. In this respect the railway of 1960 was closer to its Victorian predecessor than it was to any kind of 'modernized' service. There were other strange anomalies in training, for instance the issuing in 1957, to all the footplate staff, of a good quality hardback book entitled *Handbook for Railway Steam Locomotive Enginemen*, despite a decision in 1955 to rid the railway of steam traction as soon as it was humanly possible to do so.

Not all the work of the young driver Hobson was as exciting as running trains over the famous Settle–Carlisle route: it often consisted of no more than a trip to Keighley to relieve the crew of a Morecambe–Leeds service. These services were beginning to to be dieselized in the early 1960s. Initially, the turns were handled by one of the 'Cromptons' or Class 45s – also known as 'Peaks' after the first ten were given the names of famous English mountains, such as Great Gable, Skiddaw and the like – though there was a tendency to take these engines for more important turns and the duty would revert to steam haulage. Later the Morecambe services were allocated the Type 2s of Class 25 and the pinching stopped, as, in driver Hobson's words, the Type 2s were 'biscuit tins on wheels'.

The new diesels were introduced just as fast as they rolled off the production lines, which caused difficulties for the footplate crews during this transitional period, as crews often arrived for work not knowing whether they would be working with steam or diesel. This could cause other problems too. If the turn involved being relieved by other crews, as many were at that time, there was always the possibility that they did not have the requisite traction training. This could mean delay to the train whilst a trained crew was found, the original driver being asked to continue and provide the fresh driver with traction knowledge; even exchanging engines was a possibility, all of which had a demoralizing effect on the crews, not to mention the effect on passengers of the ensuing delay:

You did not know what you were going to get: I used to go to work in my diesel outfit but take my overalls, and a hand brush (a vital item on the footplate of a steam engine) stuffed in my snap bag. This was right at the end at Old Oak, but it used to happen at Manningham, just not as often. What was happening at

Looking much the worse for wear, though probably less than six years old, Class 9F 92067, with a train of empty flats, threads her way out of Kingmoor yard onto the main line.

Manningham was that all that summer, before I went to Old Oak, I was firing all the time and then when it got to winter it was back on the shed cleaning. It was this which set me off looking round for somewhere else, really what led to me going down to Old Oak in 1963.

(driver Hobson, 1995)

And R.M. Tufnell puts it like this:

BR were faced with a tremendous task for, whilst continuing to maintain the steam fleet, it was necessary to train thousands of staff in the new techniques demanded by the maintenance of a growing diesel fleet. At the same time thousands of footplate staff had to be trained to handle the new locomotives; separate training was needed for each type since they varied widely in almost every detail.

(Tufnell, *Diesel Impact*, p. vii)

Another effect of modernization was that there were constant changes being made to the allocation of locomotives to various depots and duties; engines designed to work the fastest express services found themselves being allotted more prosaic tasks, such as parcel trains, empty stock workings and lesser passenger turns such as cross country, stopping and semi-fast services. Though this aspect of modernization may well have provided an enthusiastic young footplateman like driver Hobson with undreamed of opportunities, it did little to improve the lot of the average railwayman and all too often served only to further demoralize men being forced to alter the working patterns of a lifetime.

Many 'top link' drivers in 1960 had started their railway work around the time of the 'Grouping'; they had spent thirty or forty years working with steam, including as many as fifteen or twenty of those years as fireman or passed fireman. Modernization meant that these men, many with only a few years left to serve, were being trained in new forms of traction simply because of the way the link systems were organized and the manner in which dieselization was introduced. The change over to dieselization was ill thought out and used untried

York-based Green Arrow *No. 60929 in charge of an engineer's train sidles down the goods road at Leeds City station. Though the engine already carries the warning flashes for the overhead electrification, the top lamp bracket has not yet been lowered to conform with safety requirements.*

and unproven technology, which generally failed to produce better performances than were possible using steam traction. The footplatemen involved had no control over these events, on which, moreover, they were never properly consulted:

> I remember booking on one day to work the Morecambe 'Resi'. I'd just had the boiler training and we had one of the 45s. Well this old driver I was booked out with was in a right state. He'd had the five-week diesel school routine and in theory he was traction trained, but he really wasn't too sure of himself and he was having terrible trouble trying to get the engine started. I wasn't too keen myself, to have a diesel – I'd never worked the boiler in service. Well we pulled, pushed and twiddled everything, but still no go. I was sent to tell the foreman we couldn't get the engine going. I've never seen anyone look so relieved as that old driver when the foreman told us to take the spare engine – I was glad too, even though it meant a hard day's shovelling.
>
> (driver Hobson, 1995)

It is little wonder that the railway's public image plunged to an all-time low. Some classes of diesels failed with monotonous regularity, others were underpowered and would only deliver timings as good as those of the steam locomotives they replaced if the overall loadings were reduced or multiple locomotives were used. To men with years of service and a pride in doing their jobs well this sort of working environment was disheartening to say the least. The following remarks, firstly from one of Groome's interviewees, a Euston driver, and then from Groome himself (who was of course an engineman at Nine Elms and Waterloo), illuminate the footplateman's view of what was happening to him:

> 'They took men from a job that they knew everything about, and pushed them through a training school – from being 100 per cent confident, they went to 100 per cent unconfident – the status of the job went down because this was proof that knowledge was not required.'
>
> From this period the average driver lost the power and status that accrued from having the total knowledge of his machine. From this point began the greatest decline in satisfactory status and safety that enginemen were to experience since the 1880's.
>
> (Groome, *Decline and Fall*, p. 71)

Despite the lateness of the hour and the difficulties being created by the way in which the processes of change were being carried out, there were still those railwaymen who were determined to pass on their skills and knowledge to the new generation of which driver Hobson was a member. Ivan Maltby taught him the basics of firing a 'Derby 4', for example, and Jack Foster taught the passage of steam, which is a kind of shorthand for 'what happens from the moment when you lift the regulator lever on the footplate to the exhaust leaving the chimney top'.

The men who taught driver Hobson his craft, like those who were the subject

Posing in front of Class 3 Standard No. 77010 is Manningham driver Clifford Hicks. Driver Hicks was not only tall and slim, he had very large feet, a factor which he found made life hard when trying to operate the driver's safety device on the diesels. Driver Hicks came off the main line and took shed duties rather than work on the diesels.

of Wallis' book *Men of the Footplate*, had more strings to their bow than driving steam engines:

> Jack, Jack Foster, he used to be in the Navy, or he'd done National Service in the Navy: he was into the engineering side of things and he built from scratch an A1 No. 60113. It was immaculate in every detail, perfectly proportioned, 3.5 inch gauge I think it was. Another lad, Pete Dyer, was an amazing artist: oil painting was his forte – he did a really nice one of Jack's engine.
>
> (driver Hobson, 1995)

The first two years of driver Hobson's railway career, spent at Manningham, saw him at work firing mostly in and around the West Riding, across to Morecambe

Driver Jack Foster of Manningham, mentor to the young driver Hobson and builder of the 3.5 in gauge model of No. 60113 Great Northern. *The location is Bradford Forster Square station and the locomotive is one of the Fairburn 2–6–4 Ts used regularly on the Bradford–Leeds services.*

and over the Settle–Carlisle route: 'pure bliss' were the words he used to describe this introduction to footplate life. Working alongside men, many of whom were thirty or more years his senior, men intent on keeping alive the traditions of their ancient craft, the young driver Hobson was keen to hear and make sense of all they were trying to tell him. It was 'trainspotting for pay' – work was neither drudge nor chore, the only less than 100 per cent enjoyable aspect being the occasional turn on a diesel (in 1962 there were still six more years before the final steam working on British Rail, though as it turned out driver Hobson was to see steam again during his spell at Neville Hill depot during the 1970s and 80s).

The skills that driver Hobson learned from Ivan Maltby came into play much sooner than he imagined:

That first summer I got booked out one Saturday to work to Morecambe if required. I was pretty excited at the prospect of working a short-rest

Hughes' Crab 42836 rolls past Manningham MPD with the 'Carlisle Goods'. Though this particular working was not a Manningham turn, Manningham men did work Carlisle-bound freight trains and the young driver Hobson had his share of these turns.

Morecambe but when I booked on and went to the board to see what engine we'd got my heart sank – not the black five I expected, nor even one of our two 'Crabs', but a 'Derby 4', an unsuperheated Class 4 freight engine to run a passenger train to Morecambe. They blew off at 180 psi and the brakes would start to go on at 140: my heart was in my mouth. We were train No. 6, so there was no guarantee that we would actually go – it all depended how many people turned up at Foster Square. Well to cut a long story short we did go, and that old 'night fighter', as we used to call the Derby-built 4Fs, steamed like a good'un.

(driver Hobson, 1995)

(Short-rest was a turn where the crew booked off-duty at their destination for less than twelve hours before working their train back to the home depot. It was most commonly utilized in working seaside excursions and charter trains such as football specials.)

By 1964, however, the situation at Manningham was becoming less than promising. Several of driver Hobson's fellow passed cleaners had transferred down to Gloucester, to stay with steam and to try and remain on the footplate in the face of the ever mounting numbers being made redundant. Instead of moving with them to Gloucester driver Hobson chose Old Oak Common MPD in north-west London. Initially he had imagined that the steam would last at Old Oak; in the event the Western was in the van of dieselization and steam turns at Old Oak were becoming few and far between, though driver Hobson did manage to get his share of what was available, often by swapping turns with those firemen who did not like working the steam engines.

Many of the steam jobs at Old Oak Common ended up by being worked from Southall, or the engines had to be taken to Southall at the end of the turn of duty, all of which added to the length of the working day. Twelve-hour workings were not uncommon: rest-day working was likewise a relatively common practice. In the mid-1960s the London area held attractions other than a railway life: Eel Pie Island, Middle Earth, Kings Road, Chelsea and Flower Power all began to blossom during this period, for driver Hobson (who was eighteen in 1964) no less than for other teenagers. The long and unsocial hours of the railwayman's lot were often a major source of conflict, with the desire to indulge in the social activities being enjoyed by one's peers – going to Middle Earth and listening to Pink Floyd – versus a night on the ash pit cleaning fires and emptying smokeboxes: do I hear no contest?

> When I first got a steam turn at Old Oak it was on a 69xx. I'd never had any experience of Welsh coal, it had all been Yorkshire hards at Manningham – I blacked the fire out and we had to get another engine. But those Old Oak drivers were good enginemen and they enjoyed showing me how to go about things on the GWR. There was Len Hughes, a real Cockney type. I remember him telling me, on a turn with one of the Castles, 'On these engines you're just a bloody fuel transfer system.' He wasn't joking, and even with good Welsh coal and a good mate like driver Hughes, you seemed to spend all the shift with your head down shovelling.
>
> (driver Hobson, 1995)

Apart from the coal, one of the most noticeable of the differences between railway life in a depot in northern England and that in the metropolis was the make-up of the depot itself – Old Oak Common was, in driver Hobson's words, 'the League of Nations: there were Cornishmen, Welshmen, Geordies, Yorkshiremen, Brummies, Scousers, men from every depot you can think of and probably a few you cannot'.

In 1964 unemployment was under 250,000. There were therefore many alternatives to railway work in the metropolitan area and as a result recruiting and keeping staff there was a very different proposition to that which prevailed in Bradford. From being a mere passed cleaner at Manningham, driver Hobson moved rapidly through the links as a fireman at Old Oak Common, though the effect of this simply reduced the already small number of steam firing turns even further.

It was during this period that driver Hobson and I first became acquainted. I

No. 4080 Powderham Castle *awaits the 'rightaway' from Paddington with a service for the Midlands, late in 1964.*

was a fireman at Nine Elms on what was then British Railway's Southern Region, and I had moved into the engineman's hostel at Old Oak where driver Hobson also had a room. Both being keen to be enginemen as well as both being Yorkies, we became pals, and because of the relative lack of steam turns at Old Oak driver Hobson travelled with me to Nine Elms on numerous occasions, joining myself and my regular mate in No. 3 link, driver Eric ('Blodwyn') Saunders, on turns such as the 2.45 am Bournemouth paper train or the 8.35 am or 5.30 pm Bournemouth passenger services. This experience was to stand driver Hobson in good stead when the Bulleid Pacifics 35028 Clan Line and 34092 City of Wells began to make their appearance on the steam specials being worked by Neville Hill crews in the 1970s and '80s.

Running trains is one part of the equation of the footplateman's life: the other is conditions of employment – such things as pay rates, holiday entitlements and even the length of the working day. It was not until 1967 that a pension scheme was introduced for conciliation grades (essentially all the railway's 'blue collar'

Nine Elms fireman Dave Wilson (the author) in the cab of 35023 Holland Africa Line. It was with this engine that fireman Wilson worked non-stop Waterloo to Yeovil and then on to Exeter and return with the East Devon Rail Tour of February 1965. This photograph was taken by driver Hobson shortly before the engine departed for Waterloo and is included in this book at his insistence: 'This is part of the record of my footplate career and you were part of that and so you should be in there too.'

staff), and yet at the same time management were telling firemen that they were no longer needed and that there would be £250 pounds for any man choosing to leave. Another scheme, introduced only a little while later, offered one-off payments to firemen to forego mileage payments, which at the time amounted to one hour's extra pay for every 15 miles travelled over 140 miles.

There are few experiences in one's working life more unpleasant than being constantly worried about the security of one's employment, especially when that type of employment cannot be found with another employer – there's only one railway.

Relative non-transferability of skills played an important part in ensuring that once in the railway industry men stayed there. Signalmen, guards and locomotive drivers, for instance, though widely believed to be watchwords in respectability and sobriety, would find it difficult to secure a direct outlet for their skills in other forms of employment.

(Revill, *Trained for Life*, p. 70)

For men like driver Hobson, doing the job was what counted; it was simply sad that it could not be done under better conditions of service. The attitude of men like driver Hobson was in stark contrast to that of the new breed of management and the change of ethos which had occurred firstly after 1953, when road transport was denationalized, and then given further impetus in 1956 with the launch of the 'modernization' programme, before coming to its full blossoming under the chairmanship of Dr Richard Beeching.

There was however one consequence of the new style of 'business management' for which the 'Beeching Boys' were largely responsible. This was a reaction against any concept of public service and even more against the idea that anyone could be in railways because they liked railways. That was 'playing trains' and it was supposed to have been a fault of past generations of railwaymen.

(Bonavia, *British Rail*, pp. 133–4)

The very attitude which brought driver Hobson to the railway was the exact opposite of that which post-Beeching management so vociferously espoused, and in the 1960s footplatemen with the attitude of driver Hobson were in the majority. If Groome's figures in *Decline and Fall* are representative, then 75 per cent of footplate crews were there because they were 'fulfilling a boyhood ambition'. Though such gulfs existed between management's views and those of the men who delivered the services, it is doubtful whether this was any worse a situation than the sorts of relationships which existed between management and men in many other industries. Railway managers had practised a policy of 'divide and rule' from the very beginnings of the railways, so the attitude of footplate crew was scarcely a matter of concern to management whose minds were, at least in theory, on far more important issues than the state of mind of their employees. (Management had not yet learned that demoralized staff would deliver a demoralizing product.)

Beeching had arrived at the Railways in 1961 and in March 1963 published *The Reshaping of British Railways*, commonly referred to as the Beeching Plan. The British Transport Commission was replaced by the British Railways Board and 'modernization' was now called 'rationalization'. The fleet of wagons and locomotives was halved between 1962 and 1968; also in this period more than 2,300 halts and stations closed, over 50 per cent of the network total, along with more than 5,000 miles of track. On the more positive side of the equation, start to stop journey times with averages above 60 m.p.h. rose from the 200 mark in 1962 to over 600 by 1965; there were also more than 6,000 miles of modern all-welded steel rails in place and in 1962 the diesel fleet (all forms) passed the 3,000 mark –

Ex-works, No. 7815 Fritwell Manor *and Hall No. 6938* Corndean Hall *stand by the turntable awaiting despatch to their depots. The* Hall, *it would seem, needs only to make the short trip to Reading, while the* Manor *carries what appears to be a Swansea East Dock shed plate – a somewhat longer trip home. The schoolboys must have been on a works pass as they appear oblivious to driver Hobson and his camera.*

pride of place going to the Deltics which had taken over the running of express services on the Kings Cross to Leeds route and those to Newcastle and Edinburgh in 1961.

Through one of those little quirks of fate, driver Hobson was working with the Deltics when they themselves had succumbed to the inevitable, superseded by newer forms of traction and reduced to secondary workings in the latter half of the 1970s. This work was mainly on the 'North Briton' service from Leeds to Newcastle or on the paper train to Hull.

The 1960s were a period of upheaval and change on many fronts: attitudes to work, leisure, unemployment and many other social and cultural taboos were being re-examined. In 1964, after more than thirteen years of Conservative

Maunsell's update of the Urie-designed S15 No. 30830, at the head of a mixed-rake, runs into Templecombe with a West of England train. Services like these were early victims of the 'modernization' programme.

government, Labour was re-elected under the leadership of Harold Wilson. Almost inevitably the change of government brought yet another change of direction in the railways, to add to those of 1948, 1951, 1953, 1956 and 1962. The new 'white heat of technology' railways reversed the policy of 'the railway must pay its way', which had been adopted back in 1956, and rejected commercial viability as the first object of railway policy.

Despite the change of government and a change of ethos the process of renewal put in place by Beeching continued. It would have been very hard to reverse the momentum of Beeching's plans, and to an extent some of the changes put in place were necessary, though they may have been less than popular. However, the new White Paper on transport not only rejected outright commercialism, it also recognized the need to reconstruct the railway's debt burden: 'Large deficits had a demoralising effect both on management and workers and it was deemed essential to eliminate these if maximum effort and efficiency were to be attained' (Aldcroft, *British Transport*, p. 159)

D9000 Royal Scots Grey *awaits departure time at Bradford Exchange station, c. 1964, with the Bradford portion of the Yorkshire Pullman. The pipeless water tank stands as a mute reminder of steam's passing. Yes, it is a gas lamp – not everything was modernized.*

Management were cynical and demoralized, partly as a result of the 'frequent and sometimes capricious changes of policy following reorganization every few years' (Bonavia, *British Rail*, p. 104), and partly because of the size of the debt; but for the footplate crews it was the effects of the debt and the shoddiness of the planning that did the demoralizing. No longer were footplatemen respected members of the community, they were the reason the trains were late and dirty, or stopped in the middle of nowhere for hours. Slowly but inexorably the status, importance and social desirability of the railway as a worthwhile form of employment was being ground down and with it went the men who ran it. The lack of public esteem was compounded, as many footplatemen have stated, by the decline in job satisfaction:

The ending of steam can only have come as an anti-climax, the drivers experienced an immediate fall in job satisfaction, no longer were the platforms crowded with enthusiastic onlookers. The 'theatre' of the footplate had ended. . . . The relative cessation of the need to display skill was noted at once.

(Groome, *Decline and Fall*, p. 57)

In the 1950s and 60s books were being produced with titles like *Ace Enginemen*, *How I Became an Engine Driver* and *Men of the Footplate*; such books eulogized the lives of the then 'Top Link' enginemen:

I have met many fine men, and enjoyed their company, at work and in their own homes. I know of no finer characters in any walk of life, than those real enthusiasts who are still at 'the Head' of many of our trains today [1953]. . . . Senior drivers of locomotive engines the world over have much in common. Their ideas, their talk of engines, their conservatism, their affection for the old and slow acceptance of the new . . . They have usually other and deeper qualities in common, for they are men in whom many daily put their complete trust and in whom their employers have absolute confidence of their ability not only to do their jobs safely and well, but to rise to the great heights of quick and accurate judgement when occasion demands.

(Wallis, *Footplate*, p. 7)

West Country class light Pacific No. 34036 Westward Ho *stands simmering at Exeter St Davids, probably awaiting assistance up the bank to Exeter Central.*

Grimy, work-stained and wearing a chalked 'T35' on the smokebox door, Philips Marsh-based Castle No. 5071 Spitfire *waits the 'rightaway' from Salisbury.*

It is little wonder that these men became disillusioned as they turned up for work to see the locomotives, which they had cherished as though they were their own, dirty, unkempt, leaking and blowing from every gland and packing – the job was turning rotten in front of their very eyes. It was these men who taught driver Hobson, and despite what was happening around them they were determined that the traditions of the job would not go the same way as their engines.

It may be difficult to imagine, in 1996, that men went to work and enjoyed the physical demands the work placed upon them, or to understand the satisfaction to be derived from battling the elements, the gradients, the load and even the quality of coal and the state of repair of the locomotive, all of which played their parts in the footplateman's daily routine – yet there is no shortage of evidence that footplate crews did enjoy their work and gained a great deal of satisfaction from it: 'The interviews with the drivers who are working again on steam engines on the "Chiltern Line", though not part of the questionnaire set, were invaluable as confirmation of the continuing presence of job satisfaction where steam engines are involved' (Groome, *Decline and Fall*, p. 35).

Imagine, if you will, the effort required to come to work each day, seeing the decline, the waste, another engine gone to scrap; couple this with the uncertainties caused by the continual round of redundancies, moves to other depots, the continuous decline in freight, which saw the job you were booked to do cancelled, day after day – the jokes and jibes about the railways falling around your ears. To the men who had been on the railways during the days of speed record attempts, who had manned the railways through the blitz, men who had watched the hopes of nationalization wither on the vine, this was what the final years of their railway lives had come to – mocked, derided, outmoded, redundant. Keen youngsters like driver Hobson, as he was then, were the future to such men, and many of them were only too pleased to be able to pass on their knowledge – though there were those for whom the whole experience had become so demoralizing that they, like their managers, became cynical and bitter. As might be imagined, some of this was absorbed by the men whose railway life was just beginning, as this

The water column at the left edge of the picture with its hose ripped off and the mountains of clinker and rubble all tell their own sad story as Battle of Britain class light Pacific 34050 **Royal Observer Corps** *waits her next turn amidst the remains of Nine Elms MPD.*

questionnaire comment from a Norwood Depot driver's assistant confirms: 'As a group [the ex-steam men] they are more critical; they are often bitter and moan a lot about the job – the ones who are about 40 or 42' (quoted in Groome, *Decline and Fall*, p. 55).

This survey by Groome was undertaken in 1985; thus men who were forty years of age then are the same generation as driver Hobson. Part of the cynicism of this generation can be attributed to the fact that they were unable to realize their boyhood ambitions to be steam engine drivers: they had the firing experience but missed out on the driving because steam had gone before they were eligible to be drivers. What also probably contributed to their bitterness and cynicism was the way subsequent changes and events further diminished their status, pay and public standing on the one hand and increased their responsibilities and the demands made upon them in terms of flexibility in working practices on the other. Perhaps even more telling is the loss of the old traditions, the camaraderie and team work, the shared hardships. Even the loss of a footplate companion has added its own burden: 'I give it 10 for boredom now – it's very hard to keep alert – it's so lonely now – worst of all on a Sunday' (quoted in Groome, *Decline and Fall*, p. 59).

In his book on the impact of dieselization, R.M. Tufnell identifies another significant factor which says much about the mood of the period of change from steam to diesel and electric, the 'momentary triumph':

> In the last five years [1963–8] the run down had been at the rate of nearly 2,000 locomotives a year, and it was a sorry sight to see most of these once well groomed pieces of machinery running about in dirty and neglected conditions. In the early days of modernization steam locomotives had often to come to the aid of diesels in trouble, in particular to assist with train heating when heating boilers had failed to function, but latterly even this moment of triumph was denied as the diesels and even boilers came to be more reliable.
>
> (Tufnell, *Diesel Impact*, p. 67)

By the end of 1964 when driver Hobson had moved to Old Oak Common only 13 per cent of passenger workings were steam hauled, and in 1965 not only did the last steam service depart from Paddington, but as if to emphasize the changes the Western Region were conducting 'speed trials' with English Electric Type 3 Class 37s. The cream of the runs were a Paddington to Exeter timing of 173 miles in 137 minutes, a Plymouth to Bristol of 128 miles in 120 minutes and a Bristol to Paddington of 118 miles in 86 minutes.

Apart from the speed trials, however, the initial dieselization of the network was not entirely the hoped-for success. If the locomotives were less than satisfactory, the planning and management thinking were even more mediocre:

> It was also unfortunate that the fundamentals of the modernization of the system did not take place before modernization of the equipment itself. Had that been properly approached first with a 'Beeching' approach, most of the lower power locomotives would never have been built; furthermore, the

The forlorn remains of No. 6023 King Edward II, *looking very much the worse for wear. Despite the sliced rear driving wheel this engine is well under way to restoration: new driving wheel sets have been cast and within the last year a rolling chassis has been seen.*

operating problems with train heating boilers could have been avoided if other regions had adopted the line taken by the Southern and changed to electric heating as soon as possible. The same thing can be said about the decision to retain the vacuum brake for mainline passenger work.

(Tufnell, *Diesel Impact*, p. 79)

Writing in 1913 about the management of the railways in the last decade of the nineteenth century, Kenny quotes from the *Investors' Summary:*

Turning to the directors, what do we find? Three thousand gentlemen – university-bred, courtly, honest, but gilt-edged amateurs in railway work; pillars of the Carlton and other aristocratic clubs; guardsmen, sportsmen, scions of ducal houses, naval officers. Now in what country but dear old England would the control of a vast organisation of national importance be confided to such mediaeval personages? Many of the directors are very old men, with an obstinate, feudal kink in their brains, who regard their men as so many industrial vassals, needing what they regard as 'wholesome discipline'.

(Kenny, *Men and Rails*, p. 251)

Lacking a name-plate or smokebox number plate, what is thought to be No. 6998 Burton Agnes Hall *awaits departure from Paddington with one of the very last steam workings. Driver Hobson was second man on the Warship class diesel No. 829* Magpie *in the background – another coincidence in view of his current home in Newcastle.*

Railway management is and always has been subject to constant criticism from many quarters. In a great many cases these criticisms can be laid entirely at the door of management; the one real exception are the constant reorganizations as a result of changes of government, and hence public transport ideology. Indeed, governmental interference in Britain's railways is and has been, in most cases, for the worse. Only legislation on issues of public safety can be said to have been benign and even in this sphere the record of both government and the railway companies is less than exemplary.

Not all forms of railway management were aloof from the footplate. Depot foremen and even the humble roster clerk in some cases exerted undue influence. Two examples from driver Hobson's career illustrate the way in which conflicts arose between the men and the lower orders of the management hierarchy.

As a passed cleaner in the 1960s the 'holy grail' was 750 firing turns – once this magic number had been reached the full firing rate was paid, even for cleaning duties. It also meant that you were issued with the full uniform – overcoat, pea-jacket, cap badge, the lot. The corollary to this was that if you were acting up as a fireman it was necessary to complete two hours at that grade to receive firing pay rates for the whole eight-hour shift:

> You had to get two hours of firing in to qualify for the upgrading to firing rate and they had a habit of giving you a job which would take about an hour and a half. You benefited from the turn towards your quota, but because the job was less than two hours you didn't get the firing rate. Sometimes you'd be sent out and the next hand, who'd be junior to you, would get a double trip Leeds job because someone had knocked. It used to get me really mad, that one.
>
> (driver Hobson, 1995)

Another junior management problem which arose was during the period of transition from the use of the vacuum brake to the use of air braking:

> Another funny little do was at Old Oak when the change to air braking was taking place. The foreman had a list of which engines had been changed over

Rebuilt Royal Scot No. 46145 The Duke of Wellington's Regiment (West Riding) *heads the Thames–Clyde Express through Kirkstall on the outskirts of Leeds. By the summer of 1964 only thirteen of this class remained in service. No. 46145 was not one of them. (photograph © R.W. Smith)*

and which jobs were booked to be air braked. Well, on this particular day when we got on the engine the change over hadn't been finished: there were no brake handles, the connections were there, the train pipes were there, but you couldn't use the brake. My mate sent me to tell the foreman, Robinson they called him, he didn't like Yorkshiremen. I went over to the office and said, 'You've given us the wrong engine – the engine doesn't have an air brake. 'It's on my list,' says the foreman. 'It has been fitted with air brakes: you go and tell your mate to stop messing about and get off shed.'

I went back to the engine and told my mate, who said, 'If that's his attitude we'd best do as we're told. Of course when we got to Paddington the engine couldn't operate the train brake and so had to be returned to shed and a fresh engine despatched, causing over thirty minutes' delay.

(driver Hobson, 1995)

The problem with adopting macho styles of 'non-railway' management was that the junior managerial ranks created friction with the labour force, and thereby diminished the level of their goodwill and support, which was an important factor in running the railways well and effectively. Junior managers putting the staff's backs up was problem enough, but whilst this was going on the upper strata of management threw out the baby with the bath water in their attempts to rid themselves of the old 'non-sexy' image of the 'public service' railway. These remarks made in 1948 by Sir Cyril, later Lord, Hurcomb illustrate how radically management practices had altered in the post-Beeching era:

. . . certainly it will require effort on the part of all concerned to break away from the authoritarian tradition of the past while preserving necessary discipline, to make the rank and file staff feel that their views on matters connected with their work are welcome and considered. Those who are required to say what is to be done will have to take pains to explain also why it is to be done . . .

(Hurcomb, Organisation, p. 24)

In his history of ASLEF McKillop adds the footplate perspective:

I could not help feeling that it must be galling in the extreme to the mentality of those usually stiff necked ones to be forced to listen to reason at last. It must be remembered that a great deal of the misery, the long hours, the inadequate rest periods that have been forced upon us had its cause in the advice and with the assistance of those in the lower reaches of the railway administrative class.

In their own little sphere very often the latter were more autocratic than their superiors, and it was no uncommon thing for the foreman at a depot to treat the men under him with a measure of severity verging at times on brutality. Favouritism was rife . . .

(McKillop, Lighted Flame, p. 161)

For footplatemen and for steam locomotive enthusiasts the changed management style which emerged at the end of the 1960s had one devastating consequence. When the last steam service was over,

> There was a complete ban on the use of BR metals by preservation societies or other bodies owning steam locomotives and anxious to organise steam enthusiasts' excursions. This was a symptom, not perhaps very important in itself, of a change of style at the centre which was felt at all levels in the undertaking.
>
> (Bonavia, *British Rail*, p. 132)

The final few years of the 1960s were very difficult ones for footplatemen. In 1965 there had been a manning agreement which, as the system continued to contract and the new technology reduced the need for manpower, began to create conflict between the footplatemen and the guards. The good old principle of 'divide and

Though this photograph has suffered a little with age, you cannot help but wonder what is going through the old engineman's mind as he surveys the gaggle of Crompton/Sulzers standing in the diesel stabling area at Holbeck in the early 1960s. The steam shed is still there but to the right of the photograph.

rule' was again being used, and there were those guards who began to taunt the firemen by telling them they were no longer needed and that their place in the cab would be filled by guards. The situation continued to smoulder and by 1967 resulted in a full-scale dispute over the 1965 agreement. In fact few, if any, industries undergoing the structural changes that the railway was experiencing have performed any better in terms of staff–management relations: in view of the changes and redundancies it is perhaps surprising that there was not more strife, especially as the job market was still relatively open.

Just as, in the early twentieth century, when 'Men are being dispensed with in the name of economy whilst others are still being overworked and underpaid' (Kenny, *Men and Rails*, p. 250), this was still very much the case when steam working on British railways ended. Men were leaving in droves, yet those who stayed were working twelve-hour shifts, rest-days, bank holidays, whenever possible, to make up for the poor pay:

> I went and watched the last day of steam at Nine Elms. From my hostel room window I watched them tear down Old Oak Common shed. The lads from the hostel were leaving one by one and I got very close to packing it in myself. The all line promotion which had come in meant I could get a move back to Leeds and the idea that I'd be able to get back up home, stay on the job and still have a

Old Oak Common MPD on the day they knocked it down. A mass of rubble and twisted girders – a very sorry sight for anyone with any regard for God's Wonderful Railway.

few mates around was what kept me going, that and the fact that I'd have wasted six years and all that knowledge from the old drivers I'd been with. I'd started on the job to be an engine driver and that was what I was going to do.

(driver Hobson, 1995)

The loss of the steam locomotive and with it the grade of fireman was undoubtedly a major upheaval in railwaymen's lives; however, far more radical changes were to come. Driver-only operation, bi-directional mainlines, flashing green and flashing double yellow signals, a new rule book and new methods of training, the continuing decline in freight working and the ending of loose coupled workings would all make their impact on the lives of the railway footplate staff. Electrically heated, air-braked trains, closed circuit television, radio telephones, the growth of the electrified lines and yet more governmental changes of direction were also destined to affect working practices, often far more drastically than the disappearance of the steam engine.

When the steam engine went, much of the railway was still controlled by semaphore signalling from literally thousands of signal boxes. Only a few stretches of line were officially classified as safe for 100 m.p.h. running, and at least in theory only one or two classes of locomotive were permitted to exceed 100 m.p.h. in service – 90 m.p.h. being the norm. I use the words 'officially' and 'in theory' because there were test trains which were taken above these limits and there were those drivers who wished to see what their new engines could do, and naturally enough they tried them out.

Despite all these changes some of the old skills needed to be retained – road-knowledge, which will be more fully explained in the next chapter, was one such skill, and knowledge of the rules and regulations also had to be maintained and even upgraded as additional health and safety legislation was brought in.

Safety on the railway has long been a major issue, and especially so for the footplateman:

For on the footplate there is one thing which stands first and foremost – ABSOLUTE SAFETY as far as human thought and experience can provide. . . you will hear something of this when rules and regulations are being spoken about. . . . Also, you will have another thing driven into your system in all probability . . . In this job a minute often means a mile . . . And in your soul the time sense is born, never to leave it.

(McKillop, *Engine Driver*, p. 15)

To ensure that the safety lesson was fully driven home McKillop makes the following observation: 'Supposing your engine, your train and your driver are mincemeat, and you have had both your legs off – grab your detonators and crawl on your stomach until you are sure that anything on that opposite road will be stopped' (McKillop, *Engine Driver*, p. 16).

For much of the period between 1948 and 1968 it was possible to believe that the railways were still the same old railways they always had been. Many of the old traditions survived, most crews still worked in links with regular mates, but

43xx Mogul No. 7317 heads an express freight working only months before withdrawal. The scene contains a number of little touches common to the period of steam's demise, including the eight-car stop sign alongside the water column and the DMU in the siding to the right of the train.

by the autumn of 1968 when workers and students rioted in Paris, and in London anti-Vietnam war demonstrations were the big items on the news, the final steam services from Preston to Blackpool and Preston to Liverpool had gone and Stanier's class 5MT No. 45110 had snorted, slipped and wheezed her way out of Liverpool Lime Street with the 1T57 excursion – 154 years of steam locomotive practice from Trevithick's first effort to Riddles' 'Evening Star' had gone. For the fooplatemen the revolution was just beginning.

As the 1960s progressed and the modernization programme resulted in the decimation of whole classes of locomotives and closed down branch line after branch line – even main lines in the case of parts of the old Great Central route between Manchester and London – railway preservation began to grow. The first of the railway preservation schemes to bear fruit had been the rescue of the

One of the survivors: pushed up to an ex-BR Standard BR2 tender U class No. 31638 bears the legend reserved for the Southern Steam Group. The locomotive eventually moved to the Bluebell Railway in 1980.

Talyllyn in 1951, but it was not until 1960 that any attempt was made to secure a section of standard gauge line for preservation. In that year two schemes did come to fruition: the Middleton Railway in Leeds was followed within months with an even more ambitious scheme – the now internationally famous Bluebell Railway between Sheffield Park and Horsted Keynes. No one in 1960 could possibly have predicted the spread of railway preservation schemes over the next two decades, and even now new schemes are surfacing for the restoration of steam-hauled services over former branch lines. Even as I write there are proposals to re-open both the Alnmouth branch from Alnwick and the Darlington to Stanhope route in Weardale for passenger traffic.

British Rail employees and footplatemen in particular have had an influential role in the railway preservation movement. It was BR footplatemen who began to raise the funds for and eventually purchased the Bulleid Merchant Navy class Pacific No. 35028 Clan Line. Former footplate crews gave their time and effort to help establish the lines and teach the other enthusiasts how to safely operate the

Looking at this hulk it is hard to imagine that this engine has been restored to operational service. No. 34081 92 Squadron *was purchased by the Battle of Britain Locomotive Society and moved from Woodhams to the Nene Valley Railway in 1976; overhaul was completed in 1994.*

line and the locomotives; a great many of them are still involved. In the mid-1960s, for example, Holbeck fireman Terry Hodgson began spending time working on the newly formed Keighley & Worth Valley Railway, and to the best of my knowledge he still does.

The list of men who became involved in this aspect of railways whilst maintaining their own national network careers is a long one, but some of them deserve a mention. From Eastleigh works there was Harry Frith with his expert knowledge of welding techniques on the Bulleid boilers, R.H.N. Hardy and his 'Top Shed' experience, rank and file footplatemen like Brian Gibson who have combined their railway preservation activities with charitable work – Brian pioneered the 'Feel of Steam Experience' for the blind. There are men like Clive Groome, whose career seems to have come full circle as he now provides traction training to BR's own footplatemen, who need steam refresher courses before working steam specials over the national network. Driver Hobson too has put his time in on the preserved railways, having done a number of turns on the fledgling

North Yorkshire Moors Railway during the 1970s, until work and growing family commitments reduced the time available.

Footplatemen were not the only grades involved in the preservation movement: almost every department of railway operations had motivated personnel who gave time and effort to the railway preservation cause – for many this was their way of keeping the steam locomotives they loved operational well after their displacement from providing motive power on the national network.

CHAPTER 3

The Missing Link

One of the earliest changes to come about through the process of dieselization, and one which made a huge impact in an important area of footplate life, was the ending of the link system for firemen. The fireman was no longer required on many turns; indeed, in the summer timetable when train heating boilers were not required, most services ran without firemen. It was this feature of the new technology which was behind the railway management's decision to offer firemen a lump sum payment of £350 to sell their Stars – their entitlement to mileage payments on turns of more than 140 miles – if they were taken off a mileage turn, as was the case when train heating was not required.

> Quite a lot of blokes lost money with this one. I remember some lads coming down to Old Oak Common from Blyth, they'd sold their Stars on the way down, they'd no idea how much mileage they'd be losing on the Bristol, or Birmingham, or Cardiff and back jobs. This was how it was, any way that pay could be cut down they'd find it.
>
> There was another way this caused us problems. We'd be taken off our Bristol or Cardiff or whatever, because there was no train heating, and we'd be sent out with some young hand driver on a cross-London freight. The driver would want twelve hours in – for the money – but us firemen, those of us who didn't sell our Stars, we didn't want to do twelve because we were getting our mileage payment and so if we worked twelve hours we didn't get any more pay – we were working for the Queen.
>
> This caused quite a few problems and arguments. I mean, who wants to work for nothing – sometimes you did it just to keep the peace but it certainly didn't make the job any easier.
>
> (driver Hobson, 1995)

Long hours are endemic in the British railway industry and numerous official inquiries, select committee reports and royal commissions have drawn attention to the fact that long hours of work are not only detrimental to the health of the employee, they also constitute a safety risk. Working excessive hours has, beside the increased wages of the worker and the increased risk factor, another effect – one which helps to mask the poor levels of investment: it shows up as an increase in productivity. As Bagwell notes, 'The productivity of BR's labour force owed a good deal to the fact that the hours worked were

0P02 is one of the Old Oak Common's empty stock diagrams, of the type driver Hobson would have worked during the summer months when train heating was not required. The locomotive is one of the notoriously unreliable North British Type 2s. The oppo in front is fireman Hobson of Old Oak Common.

longer than on any other of the European railway systems' (Bagwell, *End of the Line*, p. 59).

Excessive numbers of hours on duty is only one aspect of the unsocial conditions which helped to set the footplatemen apart from other sections of the railway industry and from industry at large. Footplate work could begin at any hour on the clock; as a result, this often meant that footplatemen socialized only with other footplatemen – few other workers clocked on at such bizarre times as, say, 3.43 am or 6.23 pm. Having regular mates was a partial compensation for the awful working hours, but breaking up the link system, closing depots and having crews sign on for duty in rooms on the railway station all played a part in undermining the relationship which existed not only between regular mates but even between crews in different links, and thus served further to undermine one of the traditional compensations of footplate life.

The mess room, the banter, card schools, gossip and tales from other parts of the network all suffered or disappeared altogether as the new working arrangements were introduced. The shed with its bricks and mortar connections to the past, the scores of men whose jobs kept the steam locomotive active, the pot-bellied stove and the 'Oldham' water boiler were on the dole, sold for scrap and reduced to rubble, the land sold off to housing development or office blocks – creating visible change to match the relocation and technological innovation that was taking place as the footplatemen went about their daily turns of duty.

Coloured traffic light-type signals replaced the huge, ornate, track spanning gantries of semaphore signals, dozens, no thousands of signal boxes disappeared, curves were straightened, sidings closed, whole marshalling yards went, followed by vast workshops, goods warehouses, cattle docks, coaling towers, ash plants. An entire landscape, not only of buildings, but of trades and professions went right along with them, though these would only account for one slice from the revolution's pie chart of changes.

Even after the demise of the steam locomotive the closure programme was still shutting routes. The Somerset and Dorset had closed at the end of steam in 1968, and in 1969 the Waverley route between Carlisle and Edinburgh went the same way. The railway workshops, which had for decades built and maintained the locomotive fleets, were beginning to become redundant. The last steam overhaul

'We'll mek all t' lines come t' York,' said George Hudson, and in this view over the cab roof of Gresley Pacific 4498 Sir Nigel Gresley it looks very much as though he succeeded. This type of photograph is impossible today with the electrification at York. The signal gantry has gone and so too have quite a number of the lines.

at Crewe had been completed in 1967 and by 1970 all the former railway workshops came under a new umbrella, British Rail Engineering Ltd (BREL). Almost as if to emphasize the demise of the steam railway, 1970 saw the death of O.V.S. Bulleid, the last great locomotive engineer of the old-style railway companies. Sir William Stanier FRS had passed away at almost the same moment as the last of his majestic 'Duchess' class Pacifics was withdrawn from mainline service, back in 1965.

The whole of the locomotive building and maintenance system, which ought to have benefited from the changes to motive power through new orders and maintenance contracts, failed to respond to the challenges, or perhaps were never given an even playing field on which to compete:

The staff and organisation of British Rail, particularly the workshops and maintenance shed, have adapted skilfully and, in most cases, enthusiastically to the transition, but the effect on the locomotive building industry, which should

Bath Green Park and one of the Midland 2Ps used for piloting over the Mendip Hills on the Somerset & Dorset Joint Railway. Unfortunately none of these elegant 4–4–0s survived modernization.

have prospered with all this work has been traumatic, and it has virtually disappeared, so much so that the first thirty Class 56 locomotives had to be assembled in Rumania.

(Tufnell, Diesel Impact, p. 79)

Tufnell is referring to outside locomotive builders, such as the North British Company or Hunslet, but the implication is that the railway's own workshops should have benefited; instead they had closed, one by one. The change over to diesels which had begun in the 1950s and was completed by 1968 had numerous problems and failures, and though the problems were not of the footplatemen's making they were often the ones to suffer from the effects of a programme which Tufnell describes in the following terms:

> . . . although the troubles were not all due to the diesel engines, some of these proved considerably less reliable than they should have . . . British Rail struggled on with these various types, and by accepting low levels of availability and reliability, kept most of these in service for ten to fifteen years.

(Tufnell, Diesel Impact, p. 35)

On occasions the 'troubles' caused potentially life-threatening scenarios:

> I was getting a 'Warship' ready to take down to 'Pad' [Paddington Station]; it was in the evening and the service would need train heating, the engine was D810 Cockade. I went into the engine room to test the train heating boiler, I went through the procedure, got everything set, pressed the firing button and Bang! The next thing I remember was coming to on the engine room floor as my mate was trying to pull me out into the cab. I had broken my watch, banged my head and, as I discovered later, blown the top of the boiler clean through the roof cover of the engine compartment – I was lucky I didn't blow myself up. Fitters had been working on a boiler fault and gone off the job leaving the boiler full of fuel; when I set up and pressed the test button this unburnt fuel just exploded – I went off to the hospital for a check up, and they never did give me the money to get my watch replaced.

(driver Hobson, 1995)

1968 saw the last gasps of the steam era. There was a re-run of the 'Flying Scotsman', with a specially adapted, two-tenders 4472 Flying Scotsman at the head of the train, crowds all the way and a BBC helicopter for company too. The steam locomotive and railway preservation movement was also getting under way: the Keighley & Worth Valley Railway opened for passengers, the efforts to save a section of the old Great Central Railway began in Loughborough, the seeds of the East Lancashire Railway were sown and British Railways began trials of a 'radar' speed gun to catch speeding enginemen.

For footplatemen in general and driver Hobson in particular the three years from the end of steam to 1971, when driver Hobson returned to home ground and a post at Neville Hill, were very difficult years. The loss of regular mates, the

One of the second batch of 'Warship' class diesels, D850 Swift is seen here at West London yard with a banana train. The shed to the rear of the train is a washing plant for the DMUs.

hours of tedium on locomotive ferrying turns going no further than up and down between Paddington and Old Oak Common or the occasional trip to Hither Green or West London Goods did little to further interest in a job which was becoming a bore – the 'bliss' of Manningham was now just a distant memory.

From 1968 onwards, very much as the result of the demise of the steam locomotive on the national network, there was a great deal of interchange between British Railways staff and the volunteers of the preservation movement. Preservation was an outlet for those footplatemen loathe to see steam's demise and the movement, or a least parts of it, benefited from the skills and knowledge of the full-time footplate crews. It is because of the influence of preservation and the actions of the footplatemen in relation to it that there needs to be some discussion of the relationship between the two.

Once the steam locomotive had disappeared for good from the national network the railway preservation movement began to expand. The Bluebell and Middleton railways of 1960 were joined by the Foxfield and the Severn Valley Railway in 1965, and many others followed. In 1965 *The Light Railway Guide and Timetable* listed fourteen lines under its main heading, including the still BR-owned Vale of Rheidol, Fairbourne Railway, Ravenglass & Eskdale and the lines of the Isle of Man. Under a subheading 'Other Interesting Lines' thirteen more schemes received a mention, among them the Groudle Glen, Ramsgate Tunnel Railway and the tramways of Douglas and Eastbourne. By 1976 the official ARPS *Year Book and Steam Guide* listed 512 sites, lines, locomotive collections and museums ranging from the sublime to the totally eccentric.

The entry for the famous railway scrapyard, Woodhams Brothers of Barry, in 1976, lists quite a number of locomotives which have since become stars: 35027 *Port Line*, Class 4 Standard Tank 80080, Hughes' 'Crab' 42765 and Bulleid light Pacifics 34105 *Swanage* and 34101 *Hartland*. However, despite a lapse of some twenty-eight years since the steam curtains closed, currently there are still a great many ex-BR locomotives which have yet to be restored; some may never make it.

In a public lecture given recently by Andrew Scott, the new Keeper of the National Railway Museum, and entitled 'More than Playing Trains', several sets of figures were produced concerning the numbers of objects which had been 'preserved' and the numbers of people visiting the sites where these artefacts are kept. There are some 2,500 carriages, 3,000 wagons and vans and 1,500 locomotives of all types and sizes and the Association of Railway Preservation

The clag emanating from 35027 Port Line *is entirely driver Hobson's work. Driver Hobson was having a day off from being an Old Oak fireman to accompany the author in his attempt at being a Nine Elms fireman in early 1964. The engine is being readied for a run to Bournemouth on one of the two-hour trains.*

Societies estimated that there were 5 million visitors to their members' sites during 1994.

What is most noticeable about the figures is the imbalance between locomotives and other forms of rolling stock – though as the locomotives and the men who worked them were the main focus of attention, particularly for the enthusiasts, it is no surprise that this should be the case. Finding people willing to put up money to buy a locomotive is an easier proposition than finding people to purchase coaching stock. Advertisements for the purchase or repair to main line condition of steam locomotives appear regularly in the popular railway magazines, and these advertisements carry numerous forms of inducement, often including footplate access on the restored locomotive. This alone ensures that this section of railway preservation benefits at the expense of others.

The period of growth and diversity of the railway preservation movement has its real beginning in the 1970s – although it could be argued that it actually started during Victoria's reign. The expansion of railway preservation produced a number of conflicts not unlike the rivalries that existed between the former railway companies. Whilst most of this rivalry, both historical and current, was conducted with good grace and humour, there have been notable exceptions.

Professional railwaymen have themselves been involved in the preservation movement and without their skills and enthusiasm it is highly unlikely that the preservation world would have become the tourist industry it now is. For example, a letter to the editor of the *Railway Magazine* announced, 'A fund has been initiated with the intention of securing a Bulleid 'West Country' or 'Merchant Navy' class Pacific in original condition from the scrapyard. This scheme has been formulated by members of the footplate staff at a London depot' (*Railway Magazine*, 112, no. 777, 1966, p. 47). The depot was Nine Elms and British Rail staff were prominent in the formation of the Bulleid Society and the rescue of West Country class No. 34023 *Blackmore Vale*. They were also an important part of the Merchant Navy Locomotive Preservation Society, saviours of No. 35028 *Clan Line*.

West Countries and Merchant Navies were not the only locomotives to benefit from the efforts of the footplatemen: more than 250 of them donated funds to purchase the Ivatt mogul No. 46441. These men were also a vital ingredient in the return to steam on the mainline, and many gave hours of their off-duty time to help the re-opened lines run services. Though he has been unable to act as a volunteer for a number of years now, driver Hobson was one of the early volunteers on the North Yorkshire Moors line:

When I was going to the North Yorkshire Moors line I went out on the road with amateur crews; quite honestly some of them didn't have much of a clue. They had the engine wound up almost in mid-gear before we got going – the fireboy committed one of the cardinal sins by not only firing a green fire, but doing it in a tunnel. The trouble was you felt like you should say something but then with some of them you got this attitude – 'What are you doing here anyway? You should stick with your railway and leave us to play with ours.' To be fair, though, there were plenty of good lads too, willing to learn, ready to

Rebuilt Battle of Britain class Pacific No. 34062 17 Squadron *heads a train of milk tanks through Salisbury. This engine was one of the first of the Bulleid light Pacifics to be withdrawn from service. It had gone by July 1964, three years before the end of Southern steam services.*

listen – but it's like so many other things, one or two can make it rough for the rest.

(driver Hobson, 1995)

The preserved lines themselves are idealized and mythologized, even those which have made some attempt to continue to provide a public transport function. The problem is that so many people throughout the movement have become so attached to the idealized and stylized entertainment that the lines provide that they believe this really does represent 'how the railways were'. To use a Marxist term, they are suffering from false conciousness.

The preserved line is a snapshot, one which has been taken through a tinted lens and touched up round the edges. This is not the same as saying that these

'Lambton No. 29'. Lambton Hetton & Joicey Colliery 0–6–2T No. 29 is seen here at Grosmont MPD on the North Yorkshire Moors Railway. It was on this engine that driver Hobson worked during his stint as a volunteer at the NYMR. According to driver Hobson the locomotive was part owned by Chris Cubic, a driver at Scarborough MPD.

lines are not operated professionally – for indeed to have survived and prospered as they have, a tremendous amount of professional effort and expertise has been expended. The difficulty lies not in any failure to duplicate the ambience of the stations or the authenticity of the livery or the faithful restoration of the locomotive, the real difficulty is in the perceptions and notions of what the national railway system was for those who worked on it. Having been a footplateman from 1962 to 1968 this is an aspect of railway working I can comment upon from direct personal experience.

The running of the preserved line is a performance – it is role playing on a grand scale, it is amateur dramatics, and undoubtedly it is undertaken for a fair measure of accolade and recognition by peers. However, unlike the 'real' railway it is not a place of work – except for a very few, it is not the means by which the mortgage is paid and the shopping bought; it is quite the contrary, a place of escape, a hobby and a leisure pursuit. After all, few people work voluntarily and fewer still work without pay.

The preserved railway is to an extent unique in the entertainment business, in that not only does it entertain those who visit, it is entertainment for those who are operating it. The problem is that recognizing this aspect of railway preservation undermines the myth that what is being preserved resembles the original. After all, no one is now fined for shortage of steam, failing to fill in the daily record sheet or allowing water in the tender to get too hot for the injectors to work properly, as they could well have been had they been real footplatemen.

Herculean tasks have been accomplished by the preservationists, from their role in the saving of the Settle–Carlisle route to the restoration of mechanical wrecks such as 35027 *Port Line* or 71000 *Duke of Gloucester*. These efforts have been rightly applauded and celebrated, but instead of being seen as essentially leisure pursuits they tend to become part of the sanitized, even bowdlerized, version of railway history and thus further distort the true nature of railway work. The reality is described here by driver Hobson with more than just an eye for detail:

Another away day at Nine Elms: this time driver Hobson, hand on the brake, rolls West Country class Pacific 34047 Callington *into the shed.*

P and D work [preparing engines for work or disposing of them after their turn of duty] could be a real killer. Sometimes the engines would come on shed with a box full of fire – it all had to be shovelled out, the sweat would be dripping off the end of your nose and sizzling on the red hot paddle [a long metal-handled shovel used for getting fire out of the firebox].

After shovelling the fire out, coated in sweat it was now time to do the smoke box and ash pans. To clean the ash pans you went under the engine with a long rake and pulled the ash, clinker and still smouldering coals out of the ashpan and into the ash pit. Clouds of ash billowing about and sticking to the sweat, then it was time to clean out the smokebox – the smokebox ash, which is very fine and powdery, blows about and gets in your eyes; if the engine had been worked hard and in service a long time the ash could be up to the top of the blast pipe. Sometimes as you shovelled out the smokebox the ashes would still be glowing hot just below the surface.

By the end of the P and D shift the dust and ashes would be in your hair, eyes and ears – you went home like this because there were no baths or showers. The fire irons you worked with got hot and burned your fingers, the old drivers would send you underneath to oil the inside motion and here the dust coating you had accumulated was liberally mixed with oil and grease. Having made up the fire and with the oiling all done it would be fill the tender with coal and water, trim the coal and swill down the footplate. Each P and D shift was like this, more or less, and you would do three or four of each preparing and disposing, at least six engines per shift and a minimum five shifts in the week. Sometimes the foreman would say, 'The next four on the pit are yours,' and you just went at them till you'd done. There's no glamour or glory in these turns: the only benefits were you got away once you'd done your allotted number of engines, so you sometimes got away a couple of hours early if you worked like a donkey.

(driver Hobson, 1995)

For the footplatemen, operating a real railway on a daily basis is about hard work, sweat and toil much more than it is about 'performances' on the main lines.

A further area of preservation which has seen its fair share of conflict concerns the ownership and operation of the locomotives and who should drive and fire them – even how they should be fired and driven, not only on the preserved lines, but on the lines of the national network and in the hands of full-time enginemen. As an editorial in the June 1968 issue of *Railway Magazine* admits, 'Not all owners of privately preserved locomotives have been noted for their willingness to co-operate with one another.'

Neville Hill was one of the depots to gain from the return of steam to the main line in 1971, as it was the depot responsible for the York/Harrogate/Leeds/York route and for the Leeds/York/Scarborough route used on the Scarborough Spa Express services. Driver Hobson was one of the volunteers for this work and, as a result, has had trips on an impressive list of preserved steam locomotives: 92220 *Evening Star*, A4s 60019 *Bittern* and 4498 *Sir Nigel Gresley*, Bulleid Pacifics 34092 *City of Wells* and 35028 *Clan Line*, the 'Black 5s', 5000, 5305 *Alderman A.E.*

No. 246 Morayshire *is the sole survivor of the class of some seventy or more engines named after the shires of England and Scotland and the hunts that take place in them. The Hunts carried a brass fox over the name-plate and were fitted with Lentz poppet valves. No. 246 is another of the participants in the Shildon Cavalcade, though sadly she is no longer in active service.*

Draper and 5407, the sole surviving V2 4771 *Green Arrow*, the Somerset and Dorset 7F 53808, Thompson B1 1306, 'Jubilee' 5690 *Leander*, A3 4472 *Flying Scotsman*, A2 60532 *Blue Peter* and 46229 *Duchess of Hamilton* round off a truly eclectic mix of engines worked on rail tours. To add to these driver Hobson was also involved in the movements of engines to Shildon for the 150th anniversary of the Stockton & Darlington Railway in 1975: 'We were all volunteers, the jobs were mostly Sunday workings, but what counted for us was being back on the steam, running trains – it was why I came on the job and it was great to be back doing it' (driver Hobson, 1995).

Running steam services over the national network using regular British Rail crews has been something of a curate's egg – good in parts. One area which has been particularly fraught is which locomotives should work on the main line.

My view is that steam should be spectacular but it should not be common place, and that spectacle is best provided by a superb presentation of unique steam locomotives over routes of maximum length with a profile which calls for maximum effort. Not for me hundreds of Southern Pacifics or Black Fives up and down the country on innumerable uninteresting routes of 40–50 miles. We should not trivialise main line steam, and if that means that there isn't enough work for 53 locomotives that's too bad, as we should never have allowed so many locomotives on to the main line in the first place; but having done so why perpetuate a ridiculous situation.

(letter from Michael Draper to the author, 11/3/91)

At the time this letter was written, Michael Draper was general manager of the country's leading preserved railway, the Severn Valley, an important and influential figure in the Association of Independent Railways and the Steam Locomotive Operators Association – the body chiefly responsible for organizing steam locomotive operation on the British Railway network.

Platform 4 at York as seen from the footplate of Bulleid Pacific 35028 Clan Line. *Reflected in the cab window is a photographer recording* Clan Line's *arrival.*

Contrasting styles: the 1895 record breaker No. 790 Hardwicke *receives some last-minute attention before piloting the last steam locomotive built at Swindon works, No. 92220* Evening Star *on one of the York–Leeds–York enthusiast specials worked by driver Hobson.*

For British Rail footplatemen, especially those who were dedicated steam engine drivers and firemen, the return of steam traction to the main line has been a source of enjoyment, and for some, new found recognition. There is no doubt that this has only been made possible by the concerted actions of numerous individuals within the railway preservation movement and within British Rail, though here again there have been numerous tensions and disputes. There have been spectacular successes, such as the running of 60009 *Union of South Africa* from Kings Cross to Peterborough or the 'volcanic' efforts of 34092 *City of Wells* on the Settle–Carlisle route. More recently and, perhaps, even eclipsing the return of steam to Kings Cross, were the 'timing trials' over Shap, pitting 60007 *Sir Nigel Gresley* against 71000 *Duke of Gloucester* and 46229 *Duchess of Hamilton*. The only possible and, of course, unbiased criticism of this particular event was the lack of a Bulleid in the starting line up and injector problems marring the *Duchess's* efforts to take the 'blue ribbon'.

Ranged against these undoubted success stories there are the problems created by trespass, the deaths through leaning out of carriage windows, the damage caused to locomotives by injudicious handling by employees of the national network, such as that caused to 60532 *Blue Peter*, problems with water, with trackside fires, with which routes could be utilized, which locomotive got which runs, types and availability of rolling stock and last but not least the use of diesels for train heating purposes when non-steam heated types of stock were used during the winter timetable. This latter may seem to be the ultimate of all the ironies of the return of steam to the main line, but there is one irony which is at least its equal.

Former Nine Elms driver Clive Groome has, since the 1980s, been running a course on driving and firing the steam locomotive. This course has grown from an evening class in Croydon to a complete training package which is recognized not only as a standard within the preserved railway movement, but also by British Rail, who now send their own drivers to Groome's course before they work perserved steam locomotives over the national system. The success of Groome's course is based on its thoroughness: trainees are taught all aspects of the engineman's duties, from how to make trimmings for the lubrication system, how to fire up the locomotive from cold, to the workings of all major parts. Handling the locomotive includes both vacuum fitted and loose coupled stock workings. The full set of courses of instruction lasts several weeks and its successful participants are accepted as qualified by the major railway preservation schemes.

After its initial slow start Groome's course gained in popularity and acceptance and has, during the mid-1990s, begun to spawn numerous imitators. The major problem with the imitators is that no real training is being given – 'Footplate Experience' is taking over from Footplate Training. As such there is the danger of such courses becoming little more than an excuse to spend time playing engine driver for those with anything from £60 to £200 to spend on entertainment.

The importance of a quality training scheme for footplatemen cannot be overstated, as recent changes in health and safety legislation have created a situation in which, if a driver has not worked a particular type of traction during a six-month period he must undergo a refresher course on the traction in question, whether it be steam, diesel or electric. Unless dedicated crews are utilized, organizing steam traction refreshers or having regular British Rail drivers keeping their hand in on preserved lines is going to be essential if the steam specials are to continue to run on the national network, privatized or not.

Since the ending of steam traction over the national network the grade of fireman has ceased to exist and this has had a rather interesting effect on the crewing of the enthusiast specials on the main line railway. These crews are volunteers and on occasions both men in a crew have been registered drivers. In steam days the idea of a registered driver going out in place of a fireman was a serious matter and in my own railway career I well remember the sending to Coventry and ridiculing of a Nine Elms driver who went off shed and worked a train to Bournemouth as a fireman.

In 1980 an editorial in *Railway Magazine* drew attention to precisely this topic:

Another driver's eye view of one of the steam specials, No. 4771 Green Arrow, *with one of the Scarborough Spa workings returning to Leeds via Harrogate. No. 4771 is seen here between Arthington and Horsforth.*

Eleven years have passed since the last scheduled steam service ran on B.R. and, although footplate staff with steam experience are still available in some areas, numbers are dwindling and it is likely that – from 1982 onwards – some concentration in operations may be necessary to concentrate steam workings at a limited number of depots where adequate numbers of trained staff still remain. Similar considerations apply in respect of technical staff, particularly boiler inspectors.

(*Railway Magazine*, 126, no. 947, 1980, p. 129)

Health and safety has had another effect on the firing of the steam specials. Whereas in steam days firemen could be expected to work a train hundreds of miles, Paddington to Plymouth, Euston to Carlisle, Gateshead to Kings Cross, the fireman now is a delicate flower who must be replaced after seventy miles.

The interaction between the professional and amateur railways takes place on formal as well as informal levels. Locomotives destined to work over the metals of Railtrack, or whoever is currently responsible for the permanent way, must be rebuilt and overhauled to explicit specifications; in order to ensure that the stringent safety regulations are applied, Railtrack inspectors carry out regular checks both during the rebuild/overhaul process and before certification of the locomotive as fit for main line service. Another formal requirement for the preserved lines is the Light Railway Order which is obtained from Parliament through the offices of the Railway Inspectorate division of the Health and Safety Executive.

The overall effect of both the preservation of redundant tracks and the operation of services upon them and the overhaul and maintenance of steam locomotives for use on the main line has been to create a web of formal and informal networks at all levels from the management of the Charter Train Unit and the Railway Inspectorate on one side to the operators of steam locomotives and the men who maintain them on the other.

From the footplate of 'Evening Star', at the Harrogate end of Arthington viaduct across the Wharfe valley. Ahead is No. 790 Hardwicke.

What is different between the eras pre- and post-1968 is that unlike the footplate in the days of the steam-powered railway the crew of the enthusiast special or steam charter have numerous visitors on the footplate during the course of the journey, some of whom may be given the opportunity to fire the locomotive. It is also possible that the owner of the locomotive or one of his representatives could be on the footplate. This puts the footplate crew under a level of scrutiny which contrasts sharply with the vision of footplate authority and independence enjoyed by the steam locomotive engineman pre-1968. Though, of course, in terms of actually operating the service on the main line the British Rail driver is in absolute authority and could ask to have everyone, with the exception of any footplate inspector present, leave the footplate.

Running steam-hauled charter services, once the national network had ceased to use steam traction, produced a whole range of logistical problems which on occasion produced stories akin to those in *Thomas the Tank Engine*, such as water being pumped into tenders from nearby rivers, though to be fair a great many people have put in an extraordinary amount of time and hard work to ensure that the steam services have run and in the main run well. On the subject of running well, as might be expected, the setting of new records or recording new feats of enginemanship have continued alongside this return to steam. Interesting and consuming as these trials and record attempts may be (and there is little doubt that they provide harmless fun and entertainment for a great many people including the footplatemen, who are, after all, volunteers), they are at best only fun and entertainment, and comparisons with 'how the railway really was' are tenuous. As Dave Sallery, National Press Officer of the Railway Development Society, said, 'No doubt being a steward on a *Mallard* special is great fun, but it has very little relevance to operating railways in the real world of the 1980s.'

Like the operation of the crack express trains, the steam specials involve only a very limited number of crews at a limited number of depots or locations – they are the icing on the cake of a fortunate or favoured few. On the real railway the vast majority of footplate work is involved with commuter services in and around the major conurbations – taking the nation back and forth to work.

For British Rail the enthusiast special was what came to be known as 'a nice little earner'. The estimated average cost of steam excursions in 1989 was placed at £10,600 per outing, and in 1980 *Railway Magazine* commented, 'charges for special trains for railway enthusiasts are greatly in excess of those charged for other groups' (*Railway Magazine*, 126, no. 955, 1980, p. 505).

For footplatemen operating the new forms of traction on the modernized railway there was, supposedly, a cleaner and more weatherproof environment, but it did not present anywhere near the challenge, nor did it provide the teamwork and comradeship of the steam locomotive footplate. This team spirit is one aspect of footplate life which preservation has managed to maintain. The recognition of the ability of footplate work to generate team effort is widely recognized: the Ford Motor Company sent management-level employees to Clive Groome's Footplate Days and Ways course as part of their team-building programme. Thirty years earlier, writing of his experience of becoming a footplate man, McKillop commented, '"what concerns my mate also concerns me" could well be the motto printed in the cab of every railway engine' (McKillop, *Engine Driver*, p. 25).

Mention has been made of the various methods of training employed on the railway. Before1968 this was essentially 'in service' and characterized by 'self help'. The self help took several forms, the most important of which was the mutual improvement class or MIC. The demise of the steam locomotive, the decline in the numbers of men employed as footplatemen and the replacement of the engine shed with the booking on-point and single-manning all meant declining numbers of MIC classes and reduced opportunity for 'in-service' training or the passing on of other essential information and knowledge. And yet changes to conditions of employment and restructuring of grades, coupled to the new working practices brought in by the modernization of the traction fleet, created the need for a training programme which would be able to produce an engineman from scratch.

Becoming a registered driver involves two separate forms of examination. One tests both knowledge of the rules and regulations and knowledge of one or more forms of traction, be that DMU, diesel or electric locomotive. The other tests knowledge of the route over which he or she will work trains. Before commencing on the process of route learning the trainee must pass the former examination.

Two ICI25 power cars at Derby, where they had been sent for maintenance. This photograph was taken on a snowy day by driver Hobson during his time on the MP12 course.

Historically the onus to pass these exams was very much on the individual – no official training was provided – but in the 1970s all that changed. Driver training simulators had been introduced in 1965 and by the mid-1970s the new thinking was embodied into a course of instruction under the heading MP12.

Driver training schools had been set up in the 1960s to teach the men what they 'needed to know' to operate the diesels. These were essentially traction training courses and they typically comprised a five-week basic course with courses of less than one week duration on the different types or classes of locomotive or multiple unit. These one-week courses were more familiarization than training *per se*. They did not teach rules and regulations and thus did not fulfil the need for a supply of trained secondmen or driver's assistants ready to fill vacancies in the driving lists. New health and safety legislation was also creating a need for basic safety training to be provided, and so the MP12 Driver Training programme was introduced in 1977. The course was composed of both practical and classroom work; there were five weeks on the rules and regulations, nine weeks' basic traction training, three weeks' route learning technique and ten weeks train handling with a diesel instructor.

Driver Hobson was one of the first to undergo the new training course, for despite having been on the footplate since 1962, he was still a fireman in 1977. When he moved back north to Neville Hill from Old Oak Common in 1971, he had gone from being a link two fireman to next but one youngest hand at Neville Hill, and thus only gained sufficient seniority to make driver in 1977, fifteen years after starting as a cleaner.

The MP12 course was a bonus to driver Hobson, because of his enthusiasm, long service, attendance at the MIC and even participation in the social life of the MIC. However, as he himself would be the first to point out, 'In this job when you think you know it all that's when you'll screw up and make a mistake' – a lesson handed down from generation to generation on the footplate. Thirty-four years into his railway career driver Hobson still maintains this attitude as part of his daily working philosophy.

> One of my mates at Old Oak, Phil Meakin, had just got his papers to get ready to go and pass for driving when I got notification of my move back to Neville Hill. I'll always remember the date because I'd been best man at my mate's wedding on the 1st of May and I had to report for duty at Neville Hill, May 10th 1971. If it had been a couple of months later I'd have been passed for driving at Old Oak before I moved back. As it was it was four years before I got to go and pass at Neville Hill and then when I was due to go I got put back nearly a year because of MP12 coming in and I got the impression they wanted us to be sort of like guinea pigs.
>
> (driver Hobson, 1995)

The in-service training which had been the hallmark of footplate practice for over 150 years was about to be replaced by a taught course. As has been mentioned, the course was divided into four sections and began with the five-week rules and regulations course. A knowledge of the rule book and sectional appendix to the

Old Oak Common after they'd knocked it down and built it up again. This is the view from driver Hobson's room in the engineman's hostel at Old Oak Common Room 225 E corridor. The motive power is an eclectic mix of Western Enterprise, Warship, Hymek and Brush Type 4.

working timetable is still a vital part of the engine driver's knowledge. The rule book has been an organic production, formulated over many years, incorporating the recommendations of the Railway Inspectorate and other safe operating practices built up as a result of operational realities in everyday service. Would-be drivers are examined on their knowledge of the rule book and are regularly tested to ensure that they retain their working knowledge of the rules governing the running of trains and safe railway operation.

The rule book in force into the 1970s consisted of some 240 rules, many of which had numerous clauses attached or were subject to special local considerations. The first sixteen of these were general rules; the rest were all concerned to a greater or lesser extent with the running of trains. In order to understand some of the changes that were becoming manifest in footplate life following the modernization programme a little explanation of some of the more important rules pertaining to the safe operation of trains might be helpful.

Rules 55 and 56 concern the actions to be taken by footplatemen in the event of their train being detained on the running line. These two rules cover thirteen pages of the rule book; the following extract gives some idea of the nature of the duties to be carried out:

Rule 55(a). When a train has been brought to stand owing to a stop signal being at Danger the Driver must sound the engine whistle, and, if still detained, the Guard, Shunter or Fireman must go to the signal box and remind the Signalman of the position of the train, and, except as provided in clause (d), remain in the box until permission is obtained for that train to proceed. In clear weather a train must not stand more than two minutes at a stop signal before the man goes to the signal box but during fog and falling snow the man must at once proceed to the signal box.

Should however the conditions of clauses (f), (g) and (h) and Note 1 be applicable the instructions contained therein must be observed.

(British Rail, *Rules for Observance*, p. 55)

On today's railway this set of instructions is utterly worthless: the signal box could be thirty miles away and the train may well be operating without a guard or fireman. However, the rule still has to be carried out: it is the method by which it is carried out where the changes have occurred. Today the driver would contact the signalman either by trackside telephone attached to the signal post or, as is increasingly common, by the cab to cabin radio telephone. At the time the rule book quoted was current some signals were already covered by track circuit and there were those with telephone too; the reference to clauses f, g, h, etc. are in fact references to these anomalies or exceptions.

Another extremely important set of rules covers what action is to be taken when a train is 'stopped by Accident, Failure, Obstruction or Other Exceptional Cause' (British Rail, *Rules for Observance*, p. 174). Rules 178 to 188 cover these eventualities, or at least some of them. Between them these rules cover thirty-six pages and here again there are the same problems as with rule 55 – no guards and no signal box within walking distance. An additional difficulty is the need to carry out various forms of train protection, especially with regard to oncoming trains in the event of an obstruction or derailment. The widespread use of track circuiting has led to a new means of affording the train protection previously carried out by placing detonators on the track – though this still happens.

The first thing which is carried out on today's railway in the event of any obstruction is the placing of a track circuit clip on the opposite running line. This has the same effect as if a train were to be occupying that stretch of track: it turns the signal immediately to the rear to red and indicates to the signalman 'train on line' on his instrument panel. The placing of detonators, once the primary method of train protection, has become a secondary or back-up system.

Rules 178 to 188 also cover the procedures for working 'wrong line', and these arrangements too have been drastically altered, essentially because of the greater distances of track controlled by a single signal box and also because of the introduction of bi-directional signalling. What has not changed is the need for the driver to be fully acquainted with these rules: to ensure that he is, a system of bi-annual rules exams has been instigated. The current method of administering this examination is for the driver to sit at a computer keyboard and answer multi-choice questions. However, the initial examination to become a driver was a much more thorough affair.

The introduction of MP12 took place alongside a major revision of the rule book, thus newly trained men were examined in the new rule book, whereas the older hands who were already drivers were given a short three-week refresher course on the new rules and how the pre-existing rules had been amended.

When they did away with the old rule book, wrong line orders used to be one of the most complicated rules in the rule book. Section C in the new rule book which covers signalling and block working was going to become one of the most important sections of the new rules. If a driver doesn't know how to read signals he shouldn't be a driver. So we went into signalling and block regulations very deeply and we were examined in the same way. We were with Inspector Clem Brittain; he spent six hours questioning us on the rules and regs. Norman Antler took me on the engine at York shed. I was there six hours with an hour for lunch then another hour on the engine – I made overtime by the time we'd finished and that was only the basic traction, faults and failures.

V2 No. 60817 was one of only a few engines of this class to be fitted with a double chimney. No. 60817 is seen here turning on the Wortley Triangle, passing Wortley South Box. From the look of the exhaust and from the position of the 'dolly' alongside the rear driver it looks as though the engine has already started to set back tender first towards Leeds. (photograph © R.W. Smith)

After this came actual train handling, in my case over the York to Newcastle road. D193 was the engine if my memory serves me correctly.

(driver Hobson, 1995)

To put these examinations into some sort of context, graduates can elect to take their degrees by written exam; if they do so they sit nine papers of three hours' duration. By the time an engine driver has passed his rules and regulations, basic traction and route knowledge examinations he too will have spent twenty hours or more being examined on his knowledge of his work and the routes he is qualified to work over. This route knowledge is an absolutely vital part of an engine driver's repertoire. Knowing where you are in daylight is one thing: at night, in fog or in snow is a different matter entirely.

Formerly, route knowledge, like much of the rest of the footplateman's knowledge, was acquired in service, but the rapidly changing conditions on the

The fireman puts a few rounds on! A brace of ex-works Deltics outside Doncaster Plant.

railway meant that this area too needed to become part of the training package. Thus the years of in-service training were replaced with a six-month classroom and practice-based course of instruction conducted by footplate inspectors, traction inspectors and signalling inspectors and incorporating a driving simulator for the teaching of road learning technique. Currently there are moves to teach drivers the entire road using the driver simulator and videos of the route, although many of the railwaymen I have spoken to have expressed some degree of misgiving over this particular move away from the traditional route learning method of riding in the cab over the route being learned.

One important objection to the new method is that the camera only looks directly ahead whereas objects to the sides of the track can be of great assistance in fixing one's location: thus an area of assistance is effectively shut off by the

The 1960s electric locomotive of Type A, built to operate the West Coast electrification. No. E 3057 was built by British Railways, though several manufacturers also built versions of this locomotive, among them British Thomson Houston, Metropolitan Vickers, English Electric and General Electric. This class spans several years of production, beginning in 1960. The operating weight of these locomotives varied with the manufacturer from 73 to 80 tons; with a power output of 3,300 hp they were half the power of the Class 91s, a third of that of the TGV. These two examples are sited in what looks like a field, though it is in fact very close to Crewe South MPD.

nature of the way the camera presents the route. No two drivers necessarily use the same landmarks in their route knowledge, but they all do use landmarks. Knowing the route from Kings Cross to Glasgow via Edinburgh and Carstairs, as driver Hobson does, is a considerable feat of memory – reducing the level of information available to aid that memory, as video route learning does, makes the driver's task more difficult.

The impact of the new training methods and how they have re-shaped traditional skills and techniques will be assessed in the next chapter. When driver Hobson made the move from London back north to Neville Hill in 1971, passing for driving and MP12 were all in the future.

Driver Hobson's return to the North coincided not only (more or less) with the return to steam on the main line but also with the establishment of another new speed record. On test between Longsight (Manchester) and Willesden (London) a Class 87 electric locomotive reached 144 m.p.h. 1972 was the year that the prototype high speed train (HST) was authorized – it was given its first

Prototype IC125, a class 47 and a production version of the IC125 stand line abreast in the gathering gloom of a winter's afternoon at Paddington.

demonstration between Kings Cross and Darlington in 1973. Neville Hill crews were among the first to be given training on the HST; because of manning disputes, however, they were introduced first onto the former Great Western routes out of Paddington.

At the time the HSTs were despatched to Paddington, the basics of GWR motive power were the two types of 'Warship' class, the 'Westerns' and the 'Hymek type 3'. This latter were working services over the South Wales road, formerly the turns of Kings and Castles – little wonder that these engines were flogged to death and that the timings were no better than in steam days. The HST was undoubtedly the first real improvement on steam service timings, though a great deal had been lost in getting there, as these comments from the *Railway Magazine* acknowledge:

> whoever it was who decided to replace the Stanier Pacifics, which in relatively normal circumstances could easily develop 2,250 drawbar horse power, with the English Electric Type 4s . . . which at best could manage only around 1,650, should not have been surprised that the diesels struggled to keep the schedules north of Crewe.
>
> (*Railway Magazine*, 138, no. 1090, 1992, p. 51)

HSTs entered service on the East Coast with the 07.45 Edinburgh–Kings Cross on 20 March 1978, and by May there were eight regular HST workings over the route. Two years later, in 1980, the Deltics began to be withdrawn and Charles Timms and others launched the D9000 Fund. Across on the West Coast route the APT-P hit 162.2 m.p.h. on 20 December 1979, and there were people saying 'enough is enough' in rescuing Barry hulks.

The first phase of modernization from 1956 to the advent of the HSTs is little more than a catalogue of ignominious decline, shrinking route and track mileages, shrinking labour force, declining freight traffic and passenger numbers. The growth areas were railway preservation, job dissatisfaction and a widespread disenchantment with everything to do with British Rail – the link system was not all that was missing.

CHAPTER 4

A Clean Bright Future

In the mid-1970s, as Britain experimented with the Advanced Passenger Train (APT), the French railway company SNCF began the process which led to the introduction of the TGV, or Train Grande Vitesse. This service, which for much of the route runs on specially constructed track, away from towns, with few curves and largely following the lie of the land and thus involving quite severe gradients, was a major success. City centre to city centre journey times over distances of 300 to 400 miles were superior to those afforded by air travel, and the first TGV line from Paris to Lyon brought 500,000 new passenger journeys during the first year. Increases of traffic have been noted on numerous occasions when routes have been electrified or have had other improvements made which result in time savings – roughly speaking a ten per cent reduction in journey time is matched by a ten per cent increase in passenger traffic, more in some instances. Electrification has been so successful in increasing passenger levels that there is a widely recognized 'sparks effect'.

There was, almost inevitably, some political manipulation involved in the TGV, particularly in taking the northern route via Lille to the Channel coast and in the siting of a station in the Picardie region. In an attempt to rejuvenate an ageing industrial region, the construction of a station and other infrastructure projects around Le Cruesot can also be said to have involved political rather than strictly railway decision making. However, the decision to proceed with the TGV was based on a programme of cost benefit analysis and was characterized by what has been described as a 'medium technology solution', that is no radical new ideas were involved in the Train Grande Vitesse: the speed increases were achieved through straight track, high powered (16.500 hp), unit type trains and improvements to existing types of equipment.

In Britain the Advanced Passenger Train took a route which has been described as the 'scientific route', that is one characterized by attempts to find new technological solutions that would allow high speeds to be achieved over existing routes. In true British fashion the APT designs suffered from lack of investment and, perhaps more importantly, poor management and even outright hostility from some areas of the engineering establishment within BREL. The Italians picked up the ideas and have gone on to develop a highly succesful version of the APT, whilst in Britain one small part of the original is parked outside the National Railway Museum – a rusting object of curiosity.

1980 saw the retirement of O.S. Nock, an author and journalist who for twenty

Class EMI 76022 – formerly EMI 26022 – along with an unidentified member of the same class, pictured at Tinsley near Sheffield. These locomotives were first introduced in 1941, although they were not actually put into service until after 1950. From 1941, when the LNER constructed No. 26000 Tommy, *no engines were built until after nationalization. Driver Hobson's uncle was a driver at Mexborough and acted as a tutor driver when footplate crews were being trained in the use of these engines.*

years had written a column in *Railway Magazine* entitled 'Locomotive Practice and Performance'. The grand finale to his contribution to this long-running series was a trip on the APT on 3 October 1980, and the article appeared in the December issue of the magazine. The APT with its revolutionary tilting mechanism had already been the subject of less than favourable comment in the national press, and Nock tackled this issue head on:

The run of October 3rd was a triumphant demonstration of high-speed running, of principles in which Great Britain is now leading the world in railway engineering technology. In the circumstances it is a pity that certain organs of the press, in pursuing their cherished pastime of 'knocking' British Railways, should still be persisting with their story of a queasy ride. As the feature above all others that makes such high average speeds possible over a route including much curvature, the tilting mechanism naturally came in for close scrutiny; but any suggestion of a rough or unpleasant ride is just fantasy. The 'knockers' should watch their words because they could jeopardise, if not actually sabotage the chances of British Rail Engineering Limited securing some very substantial export business – not only selling the 'know how', but in manufacturing the hardware in large quantities.

(*Railway Magazine*, 126, no. 956, 1980, p. 575)

The final chapter will discuss further the actions of the Fourth Estate in relation to the notion of 'knocking', but for now it is perhaps sufficient to say that the APT never did properly enter traffic and that the reasons for that included not only the poor press but problems of management, engineering and government commitment.

The enormous gulf between the British and Continental methods of railway development are manifested not only at the technological, managerial and political level; they are also glaringly apparent at the employment level, as Bagwell notes: 'What was conveniently forgotten when comparison was made with the working conditions of French footplatemen was that their basic rate of pay was

The APT 'under wraps'. There is a strange affinity between this photograph and that of No. 34081 92 Squadron at Woodhams yard in Barry (p. 72).

180 pounds per week, more than half as much again as the basic rate of the B.R. driver, while standard hours of work were only 35 to 39 per week' (Bagwell, *End of the Line*, p. 93).

Eighty thousand footplatemen were at work on British Railways when it was brought into being on that first day of January 1948; this figure declined rapidly and a mere 19,000 footplatemen saw in 1980. Today this figure is closer to 14,000, and even this figure is falling. The clean bright future apparently offered by 'modernization' may have had some relevance to the improved creature comforts of the cabs of diesel and electric locomotives – though theory and practice diverged in this respect, as we shall see – but its relevance to the working conditions of the staff can, at best, only be described as tenuous, and when applied to their continued employment the only word is disastrous.

The Deltics were one of the most popular and highly praised of the diesels in service with British Rail, yet they were so noisy in the cabs that crews had to be issued with ear protectors. (Initially these were simply common or garden wax plugs, which unfortunately led to the crews suffering ear infections.) Other drawbacks included draughts, lack of reliable cab heating and sundry other minor niggles, such as the constant smell of diesel fumes: all these niggling faults conspired to make life in the cab not as comfortable as it ought to have been.

Footplatemen often complain that the HSTs, the Deltics' true replacements, are also very noisy in the cabs:

> After a round trip Kings Cross I'd be going home down the coast road, look down at the speedo and I'd be doing a ton. It was so noisy going there and back in the 125s, your ears would be singing and you just didn't realize how fast you were going. It's very fatiguing going London and back with the 125s: it's the combination of concentration, engine noise and, often worse, the wind noise, combined with a round trip of 560 plus miles – it's a lot better with the 91s, the leccy is fairly quiet and in the DVT it's almost like one of the coaches. One of the standing jokes about working on the 125s was that it was like driving to London sitting in the smokebox of an A4.
>
> (driver Hobson, 1995)

The Deltics had been in traffic for almost twenty years in 1980, and during that time had managed average annual mileages of 140,000, but this high figure (compared with the English Electric Type 4s, which averaged 80,000, and a Stanier Duchess which managed about 67,000) had been bought at a high price. Between June 1961 and April 1977 D9007 *Pinza* travelled 2,230,000 miles and in doing so it underwent no less than fifty-five engine changes, or almost three and a half per year. Engine changes on the Deltics were so frequent that an entire system was developed specially to deal with them.

The process of electrification and the provision of a modern diesel fleet had, by 1980, been under way for more than twenty years, yet as British Rail went into the eighties the East Coast route to Scotland was not electrified. There was no electrification at all on what had been the Western Region or Great Western Railway, and the former Southern Electrification was incompatible with the

English Electric Type 4 No. 40084 heads north through Marsh Lane cutting with a Liverpool–Newcastle service.

standard adopted for the rest of the network; the network itself was still essentially the same one which had been erected by the Victorians. True, there had been alterations and additions, curves realigned here, a crossover or junction taken out there, a few miles of deviation installed, improved signalling, but in essence the trains still ran over the tracks that Locke, Brunel and Stephenson built. There is a relatively simple reason why this is the case: 'the aggregate value of tax subsidies to the company car owners is about 2,000 million pounds a year, or roughly twice the amount of government support for the railway passenger. No other country subsidises car travel in this way' (Bagwell, *End of the Line*, p. 5).

Not only is the car subsidy hugely to the railway's detriment: because it is never directly referred to, unlike the provision of government funds for railway purposes, it creates a distorted view of the actual value of the railway subsidy. Thus the latter is attacked in a manner in which the car subsidy is not.

The footplateman's working conditions are to an extent determined by the level of investment, but this investment is political as well as financial. What investment has been made in a driver being ensconced in the cab of some twenty-year-old clapped-out DMU, riding over a line poorly maintained and littered with speed restrictions, and calling at vandalized unstaffed stations? Investment is also affected by the relationship between senior railway management and the senior members of the government:

> Sir Peter Parker has been under great pressure from No. 10 Downing Street to reduce the level of wages settlements, even though Britain's railwaymen are Europe's lowest paid. Being desparate for more investment if the railway industry is to survive he has hardened his stance against the claims of railway labour in the hope of keeping on favourable terms with the government. The outcome was that in 1982 more working days were lost from industrial disputes than in the previous 50 years of the industry's history.
>
> (Bagwell, *End of the Line*, p. 19)

As the 1970s drew to a close the footplatemen had, among other things, to contend with new rule books and new traction in the form of the high speed trains. These were a version or half-way house development from the APT programme, though without any of the sophisticated technology which allowed the tilting APT to reach 162 m.p.h. on the Beattock–Lockerbie section of the West Coast main line. However, the really radical change which the footplate crews had undergone was the new methods of training on the one hand and the alterations to recruitment to the footplate grade on the other:

> For more than a century the line of promotion to driver had been clear, but restricted. The aspiring express driver would start his railway career as an engine cleaner and proceed by (often prolonged) stages to the various grades of fireman and engine driver. Revolutionary changes in railway technology made many of the old grade distinctions meaningless. Under the trainman concept these rigid lines of demarcation would be removed and promotion onto the footplate would be possible from other grades in the service.
>
> (Bagwell, *End of the Line*, p. 91)

One plank in the Conservative election strategy in 1979 had been to make a play on the relationship between Labour, labour and working. This they did in a poster campaign which proclaimed that with over one million unemployed, 'Labour isn't working'. Under the Conservatives, of course, fewer still were working. In 1982 at a special general meeting in Birmingham the railwaymen's leader Sidney Weighell commented,

> There are four million out of work out there. There are 30,000 private lorries parked against walls waiting to carry freight traffic. That is the world you live in. I went down to North Wales, down the Barmouth coast. They are frightened to death to stop in case the line never, ever, opens again. These are the stark realities.
>
> (Bagwell, *End of the Line*, p. 118)

Driver Ron Heritage, once of Old Oak Common, was one of those men tempted to travel abroad to stay with steam workings. The last driver Hobson heard of him was that he had emigrated to either Kenya or South Africa.

If the years leading up to the end of steam were bleak years for the footplatemen and the railways, the 1980s were to prove even less inviting. 1982, in particular, was the most bitter year on the railway for half a century: 'These stoppages were not haphazard ones, they were the culmination of a government of hostility to public enterprise and to railways in particular' (Bagwell, *End of the Line*, p. 83).

The ethos of public duty, upon which a great many footplatemen set a very high store, as we have seen, was subjected to a severe attack by the Thatcher government, a trend which has continued under her successor: 'The over-riding aim was to increase opportunities for private profit making in transport and to curtail drastically the role of public enterprise. This objective has been pursued for its own sake, largely irrespective of any considerations of transport policy' (Bagwell, *End of the Line*, p. 55). There could scarcely be a greater contrast between this and the views of Sir Cyril Hurcomb, in his introductory remarks to the newly nationalized railways:

> Physical development is a field in which Nationalisation has advantages . . .
>
> Again a nationalised undertaking is likely to find it easier than any private commercial enterprise to take a long view, to time its investment, to go ahead with physical development at a time when unemployment is increasing and labour is available, and thus to assist in maintaining full employment.
>
> (Hurcomb, *Organisation*, p. 23)

The public duty ethos which had been nurtured amongst the men by a great many railway companies long before nationalization, and which continued after it had been introduced, was not simply the 'job first' attitude: it was, as we have seen, part of the 'status' of the job. The picture painted by Revill in his paper on railwaymen's identity, 'To serve the railway was to serve the nation . . . to make sacrifices to the good of the nation as a whole' (Revill, *Trained for Life*, p. 71), is utterly out of step with the sentiment that there is, 'no such thing as society, only individuals and families'. With such contradictions as these it was inevitable that there would be tensions and difficulties, and after three years of Thatcherism, in 1982, the footplatemen went on strike – ostensibly over the operation of driver-only trains and the introduction of flexible rostering. However, given some of the issues mentioned above and in previous chapters, the loss of craft traditions, the demise of 'self help', the 75 per cent reduction in numbers, falling pay, reductions of status and declining job satisfaction were all equally part of the equation, all grist to the mill of discontent, as no doubt was the need to work longer and longer hours so as to be able to generate a 'living wage'. Flexible rostering was arguably more a case of the straw which broke the camel's back rather than the sole reason for the dispute.

ASLEF called for, and got, action with a series of strikes in January, February and July 1982. Despite the action, flexible rostering for guards was introduced during 1982 and the footplatemen followed in 1983. The eight-hour day, which the union had fought for over many years, and gained only at the end of World War I, was swept aside in favour of a system allowing crews to be rostered with turns of up to nine hours. The initial proposals for flexible rostering had floated the idea of a twelve-hour roster, and it was only through a process of confrontations that the compromise of the nine-hour roster was eventually reached. This roster system is still, more or less, in place:

> The way it worked at Neville Hill was something along these lines. You would book on, take a set of DMUs down to Leeds into one of the bay platforms. Then the shunter would come and you would split the train into two or three sections, before taking the first two cars on a trip to York via Harrogate. When you got to York you'd have about ten or twenty minutes' wait before you relieved Manchester men on a Scarborough job. You went to Scarborough and back to York, where you were relieved by another set of men, usually Manchester men, but sometimes another Leeds set. If the Scarborough job was a

loco-hauled one there was all the mucking about, shunting the train, running round to do; you'd no sooner done than it was time for the right-away back to York.

When you got back to York it was time for a PNB (Personal Needs Break). Then it was over to one of the bays and pick up a DMU for a trip back to Leeds via Knaresborough and Harrogate. As if this wasn't enough, when you got back to Leeds they'd have you relieve some other crew, maybe off a London job, and work the empty stock back to Neville Hill. This little lot took about nine hours and despite all the toings and froings you didn't even have enough miles in for mileage payments.

(driver Hobson, 1995)

The introduction of flexible rostering can be seen as the human equivalent of a new process that was beginning to take shape in the 1980s. A new line in management thinking which enjoyed the somewhat dubious soubriquet of 'sweating the assets' was emerging. The Network South East manager Chris Green was very much a champion of this new initiative, which was intended to make the railway and its property give a higher rate of return. It is not explicitly stated that flexible rostering is designed to 'sweat' the staff, but if, as is often claimed, the manpower resources are a company's major asset, it is implicit that they too will be 'sweated'. Professor Bagwell spells it out quite clearly: 'Labour was carrying a large part of the burden of a depressed railway industry' (Bagwell, *End of the Line*, p. 59).

On the 1970s railway, despite all the difficulties already described, there were still attempts to 'get there' and several high-speed trials were being made, both with the High Speed Trains and with the still experimental Advanced Passenger Train which in 1975 reached a new UK rail speed record of 153 m.p.h., though this was not in revenue-earning service. In 1977 the High Speed Train on a London to Bristol and return journey averaged speeds of more than 100 m.p.h., start to stop, in both directions. However, the high watermark for the HST came in 1985 with a running of the Tyne-Tees Pullman, with drivers Bob McManus and Bob Snaith at the controls, which set a new record for UK passenger train speed of 144 m.p.h. Footplatemen, it seems, were still prepared to have a go: after all, having a go on the modernized railway involved no more physical effort, unlike the speed attempts of the steam days, although the level of concentration and adrenalin might be higher when attempting speeds such as 140 to 150 m.p.h. or more.

The move to flexible rostering and the shortened journey times resulting from higher speeds simply led to further footplate redundancies. Although 1980 saw the best passenger figures for almost a decade, it did not improve the railway's operational environment, nor prevent redundancies. Much of the rolling stock and many of the DMUs and diesel locomotives were worn out, yet very few new items of either rolling stock or locomotives were being built. The railway's chief executive was desperate for investment funds – so desperate, apparently, that industrial relations were jeopardized.

Flexible rostering was followed by the intrduction of Driver Only Operations,

'York, this is York.' On the through roads stand HST No. 254010 and an unknown English Electric Type 4, first and second generation diesel power side by side.

known to the footplatemen as DOO jobs. The pressure to shed more and more labour, which had seen such huge decreases over the first twenty years of modernization, was an ever-present shadow hanging over all negotiations over pay, hours and conditions. The railway's labour force shrank by more than 30,000 between 1980 and 1985, and this was at a time when employment prospects were very poor – especially for those with the non-transferable skills of railway working. Laying off an average of 6,000 workers a year for five years would have been seen as draconian if it had happened in any other industry, but on the railway it was a little different: 'The press helped to nourish the belief that the railways were grossly overmanned and that a reduction in staff numbers was a prerequisite for improved productivity' (Bagwell, *End of the Line*, p. 83).

The role of the press in railway affairs is a subject worthy of treatment in its own right: for this narrative it is sufficient to say that the attitude of the press in railway issues is not one which could be described as 'neutral' – indeed, 'hostile' would seem to be a more suitable adjective.

One of the earliest routes to commence Driver Only Operation was the St Pancras–Bedford service. A 23-year-old diesel multiple unit service was replaced with an electrified line, modern units and innovations such as through ticketing on London Transport services, and, even more radically, driver to passenger communication. As the trains were operated solely by the driver, a closed circuit television system was used at most stations, so that the driver was able to see when it was safe to close the doors after the passengers had joined or alighted from the train.

In addition to the installation of CCTV there was a major re-signalling of the route. The description of this new system in the LMR Midland Suburban Electrification Project brochure gives some idea of how very different the environment between the old railway with its semaphore signalling and the new computer-controlled network was beginning to be: 'The modernised signalling system means that one new signal box controls the whole route and replaces 30 old boxes. A computer controlled system keeps the signalman advised of the whereabouts of every train on the route.' (West Hampstead box, which was built to operate the St Pancras–Bedford route, controls 596 signals, 328 sets of points and has cabin to cab radio telephone links.)

As well as the new practices being brought about as the result of technological change, local changes were being effected through several routes. One such change was through expanding partnerships with newly created bodies such as the regional passenger transport authorities; another was through changes to the operation of the practice of 'traditional route knowledge'. (Traditional route knowledge was not about road knowledge *per se*: it was about which depots had traditionally worked which routes and how far. Copley Hill (Leeds) men worked the Great Northern route to London, Holbeck men worked there over the Midland route. When Copley Hill closed and the men went to Holbeck the Great Northern route to London then became part of Holbeck's traditional route knowledge, and the crews then learned both roads to London. This was one way traditional route knowledge altered; another is described by driver Hobson:

> We lost a lot of work at Neville Hill when they did away with traditional route knowledge. Manchester men, 'Wessie' men or those from the old 'Clog and Muffler' [crew from either former London North Western depots or from ex-Lancashire and Yorkshire depots], who we used to relieve at Leeds on the Liverpool–Newcastle services, started running to York when they'd learned the road. We were road learning men who were taking our work. We lost all our Newcastle turns except for the 'North Briton' and I'm sure we only kept that because it started out of Leeds.
>
> (driver Hobson, 1995)

Reorganization of routes, services and the depots which provided crews and traction meant the closure of some depots and the transfer of work to others. This, to the footplatemen, meant more upheaval, more moves around the system to stay in work. It also meant that at some depots the work being covered was much more mundane. Though others appeared to benefit, it was at the expense of longer days, flexible rostering and travelling over greater distances. No longer

Liverpool or Manchester to Leeds: now it was to York – another fifty miles onto the day's work:

> I seemed to spend most of my time either going to Hull and back or round and round the York/Harrogate/Leeds circle or shuffling empty stock too and fro between Neville Hill and Leeds.
> One of the Hull jobs was the papers. We used to have about four or five paper vans and a coach with a Deltic: they'd come off the main line and we were just wearing them out. It was a bit of fun, though: with a big engine like that, a light load and nothing in the way you could be charging through Garforth at going on a ton. Though I have to say most of the Neville Hill work at the time was DMU jobs, not the most exciting of work and very little by way of mileage turns.
>
> (driver Hobson, 1995)

In the twenty years which had elapsed between driver Hobson's first day, back in 1962, and the industrial disputes of 1982 not only had the physical and visible aspects of railway work changed – the sheds, coal towers, lineside cabins and semaphore signals had gone or were disappearing fast – but the unseen and invisible aspects of the work had changed too. Increased isolation, the decreasing social value of the work and the continued slide down the pay league charts were all part of the footplateman's working reality. Despite these less than favourable conditions many footplatemen still enjoyed the job and still participated in age old practices, such as the Mutual Improvement Class and its social counterpart, the quiz night:

> The Eastern/North Eastern region did keep some of the MIC stuff going: we still had the quiz nights and the trips to various places of interest. We went to France to a TGV depot on the outskirts of Paris and saw how they were maintained. The whole train, which is an articulated set, could be jacked up as one complete unit to allow work to be done. The place was run like an office: all the work was done Monday to Friday – at the weekend everything was out in service.
> Out on the specially dedicated TGV road there were no signals. A transponder in the track lit up a series of lights in the cab: these were the signals. Target speeds would come up and if the driver didn't react to these within a set time limit the computer would take over, braking the train to within the required speed limits. The drivers were more controlled in what they could do, but they got extra pay for the TGV work and other fringe benefits, like early retirement on 80 per cent of the final wage. The ones we met were good lads, they enjoyed their work and if you saw them on the station you couldn't tell them apart from the travellers.
>
> (driver Hobson, 1995)

As the 1980s began British Rail were promoting themselves by using Jimmy Savile to tell the nation that 'this is the age of the train'. As this letter to the *Railway*

TGV unit No. 53 undergoes a serious overhaul: the whole unit, which is articulated, is lifted on synchronous jacks. The edge of the leading bogie can be seen in the lower left of the picture, with the second bogie visible under the driving trailer. The depot is so big that workers use bicycles to get about.

Magazine illustrates, it was perhaps not the best choice of campaign slogan: 'Sir – Jimmy Savile is wasting his time and B.R. money telling people what most already know, that it is the age of the train that causes delays due mainly to failures of DMU stock and locomotives which have mechanically seen better days' (*Railway Magazine*, 129, no. 953, p. 539).

By 1985 the sales slogan had become the even more disastrous 'We're getting there', and industrial relations had further deteriorated. British Rail were claiming £200,000 in damages against ASLEF and the NUR for their taking strike action in sympathy with the miners. Despite this contretemps staff productivity rose by 4 per cent, British Rail ended its recognition of the 'closed shop', the authority to begin the electrification of the East Coast route was given and in continuing trials the APT averaged 103 m.p.h. for the whole Euston–Glasgow journey.

Throughout much of the 1980s the mainstay of the East Coast express services were the HSTs and the financing of much of this fleet was greatly assisted by loans from the European Investment Bank: almost £37 million in 1978 followed by a further £25 million in 1980. Despite the investment from outside agencies, complaints of overcrowding on the HST services have persisted, though this is in part due to the problem of utilizing the unit type train – where adding extra coaching at peak points or periods is virtually impossible. Despite the crowding and other technical difficulties the HSTs did give substantial improvements over the steam era timings, something which many of the previous forms of diesel traction had failed to do. Though these trains may have brought an improvement in journey times and in levels of availability, from the crew's point of view they offered a noisy and uncomfortable working environment, like the Deltics, in complete contrast with the design and marketing brief put before the public, which described a 'futuristic and exciting' solution. The enormous gulf between the steam driven railway of 1962 and the new railway that was emerging in the 1980s is encapsulated in these remarks about the thinking behind the creation of the High Speed Train:

The wedge front and driver's cab of the 'exciting and futuristic' IC125.

The possibility of travel as a distinct and pleasurable experience has always been at the heart of the great romance with railways that made it such a powerful function and symbol of people's lives. The challenge to recreate this possibility now faces designers in developing new concepts and imagery that will not only be economic, but will also capture the imagination of the public by providing a genuine alternative in terms of quality of experience.

(Whitelegg et al., *HSTs*, p. 182)

The manipulation of imagery, so redolent of the 1980s and '90s, was still in its infancy in 1962. In the 1980s, it reached new levels of cynicism and was paralleled by changes to the operational aspects of the railways, which when seen together constitute a marked shift in the view of the role of the railway from that which was commonplace in the 1950s and '60s.

In Britain, high speed rail developments and new line construction have to be seen as a remodelling of the traditional railway operation to make it a high volume, trunk-haul service with high profitability potential and hence good potential for privatisation. This is a 're-commodification', or repackaging of rail

Lined up and ready to go. France's 186 m.p.h. 'go faster', the TGV. Another version of 'futuristic exciting design'?

services, foresaking the traditional concept of public service so that they behave instead more like high volume, uniform standard, consumer goods which can be neatly packaged as an item for sale in the eventual return of railways to private ownership.

(Whitelegg et al., *HSTs*, p. 209)

There is a tendency to ignore the effects of all these conceptual and presentational changes on the staff. Change, which is often seen from the outside as not only being desirable but even essential, can be perceived by those affected by the changes as an unwanted intrusion into their daily life by people and ideas over which they have no control or input. Frequently this intrusion is made by people who have no appreciation of the actual conditions and as a result fail to comprehend the true nature of the problems which their solutions and plans create:

As I explained about the situation at Laws Junction, what has happened is that the timings have become so tight, especially at some of the passing points, that it takes very little to put you well into arrears. Just the other week was a case in point. It was at Waverley Station in Edinburgh, I'd just had the buzzer from the conductor and opened the controller, we couldn't have reached more than two miles an hour and somebody pulled the communication cord. Some chap, a little the worse for wear, had to make an emergency visit to the toilet. Instead of getting off the train first he went into the onboard toilet and was still there when we got the right-away, and so to ensure being able to disembark he pulled the cord. A minor incident, no damage done, but by the time everything had been sorted out nearly ten minutes had elapsed. By now you've lost your path, so to add to the already late departure you may get signal checks because slower trains have been allowed to depart in front of you to avoid delay to them, as a result of your lateness, which often continues to build up.

Because everything is so tight and you have to run up to the limit all the time you simply can't get the time back. If you're late and you're a connecting service then other trains can be held. I was held forty-five minutes only the other week, again at Edinburgh; this time a train coming down from Aberdeen was held up by bad weather, my train was the connection and so we waited. People who make statements about making trains run on time do so through ignorance. No driver wants to run late: either you are missing your meal break or you are getting home late, and then people are worrying about you.

The thing with the connections is all getting out of hand. One new idea is to wait for connections only if you are the last train, otherwise it's just go when it's time – this does not seem to be the way forward.

(driver Hobson, 1995)

No amount of Citizens' Charters or fines can deal with incidents, like those referred to, which create the delay. I was recently given access to the cab of a Class 91 for the journey between Newcastle and Glasgow and return, so that an appreciation of the difference between the steam footplate and the electric's cab could be gained at first hand. On this journey there were two incidents, both of which resulted in some delay. One was the work of vandals throwing things onto the tracks. The train was brought to a stand and then ordered to proceed through the section at caution keeping a lookout for any obstruction – a length of heavy duty electric cable had been thrown onto the lines. Along this particular stretch of line incidents of vandalism are common. The children who stand on railway bridges today are not taking numbers but sniffing glue, waving V signs and throwing things.

The environment in which the footplate crew of the 1980s worked was a much more hostile place than that enjoyed by steam crews in the 1960s. The sweated assets syndrome was extended to the timings of the services – another turn of the screw, additional pressure on the drivers, who of course have to explain their lateness. Railways have become an easy target for increased levels of vandalism, and they have also been the scene for rising numbers of suicides. Driver Hobson has had people throw themselves under his train:

> When it happens there's nothing you can do: you cannot slam the brakes on and stop. When it's over every time you go past the spot you think, just for a second, even though there was nothing you could do you still have this momentary, involuntary, recall. Sometimes it's not suicide. I hit a lad running across the tracks to get away and another driver I know hit two kids. Instead of running over the tracks the little kids ran between them. He just had to sit there, brakes full on, watching in horror as he caught them up and ran over them – he broke down and left the job after this.
>
> (driver Hobson, 1995)

The parents of the dead children called the driver a 'murderer' for not stopping. This was their ignorance in not knowing how difficult and different it is stopping a train compared to stopping a car. Naturally enough this served only to further upset the driver. Though such events as these seldom feature in accounts of footplate work, they are an ever-present reality in the working lives of the footplate crew.

In addition to suffering the very real trauma of being involved in someone's death, footplatemen are immediately taken off duty and 'medicalized'. They are asked for blood and urine samples so that they may be tested for drink and drugs – though of course such incidents were not of their making. Though there are undoubtedly very good reasons for acting in this manner, some footplatemen have felt that they were being seen as criminals or wrongdoers despite their unquestioned innocence. These sorts of issue are yet another of the unseen pressures of footplate life in the 1980s and 90s. In steam days, particularly in very hot or humid conditions, it was not uncommon for crew to slake their thirst and prevent the very real dangers of dehydration with a pint of beer – today such action could well result in dismissal and imprisonment. The problem is that the modern driver's pay and conditions do not reflect this increase in the level of responsibility.

The modern footplateman works in a 'safety critical' environment; he carries with him, at all times, an identity card – his permit to be in the cab – his driving licence. If he has to leave the cab and descend to track level he must wear a high-visibility vest 'at all times', and there are now some areas where he must not descend to track level at all, as safety clearances are below new health and safety guidelines. In these new circumstances all communication is via a cab to cabin radio telephone.

So much of the old railway work has disappeared it is almost a new occupation. However, despite the enormous degree of change which has undoubtedly taken place, some of the old skills still cannot be abandoned or significantly changed:

> I learned the road in the same way that all the drivers before me had learned it. Picking out the landmarks, making notes, travelling the route, taking note of what the driver was doing, where he was shutting-off, what was he using for his braking marks and so on. I learned the road like it was in steam days, all the gradients; I even know all the old cabins. When I drive the leccy I still think it through as if it was a steam engine. This bit's down hill so I can shut-off here, coast round to the next speed check and then open up again just as if I was doing the run with an A3 or 4. I use the road to help me run the train.
>
> Knowing the road is vital. You can bluff your way through in daylight, but in the dark or the fog, if you don't know the road you might as well pack it in. When I went from Neville Hill to Gateshead I went in the spare link and spent months out road learning. In the spare link you were signed up all roads and all types of traction – 'trekkies' – boldly go anywhere with anything.
>
> When I'd signed the roads I started by doing about four or five months where I was going to London and back twenty-four times a month and maybe doing a couple of Derby jobs on Sunday workings. This was all with HSTs, not the 91s. Five London and backs were getting on for three thousand miles, lots of them at over a hundred miles an hour. It was very demanding, but that was the job now. In the old days it was London and lodge, but not any more. Though there have been rumours that lodging might be re-introduced, maybe we'll be doing Newcastle–Paris, or Brussels and lodge. Nobody seriously wants to go back to it but the way things are you never know.
>
> (driver Hobson, 1995)

Keith Tomlinson, former footplateman, now the Driver Training Manager for Regional Railways North East, explains it thus:

> every Driver on the system has to certify his/her knowledge of any route they drive trains; this is done on a special card, and to obtain this knowledge, they have to 'learn the route', by the different methods employed. The knowledge is of line speeds, curvatures, viaducts, bridges, stations, signals, etc, and is a very important part of a driver's role. All types of conditions have to be considered, such as fog, falling snow and darkness; there are no headlights fitted to trains, like cars, so it has to be a thorough knowledge.
>
> (Tomlinson, Introduction, App. 2, p. 4)

Speed trials continued unabated throughout the 1980s. In 1985 an HST was run at 148.5 m.p.h. in 'bogie trials'; four years later electric traction pushed this to 161.7 m.p.h. though again this was not in passenger-carrying traffic. Whilst this emphasis on improving services through increased speed provided the public façade, behind the scenes extra pay and inducements were having to be offered to recruit and retain staff in the Network South East area: even with mass unemployment, railway work was highly unpopular, especially the Inner London area suburban workings.

The unpopularity stemmed from low public esteem, poor pay and a poor working environment. The attitude fostered by post-Beeching management, of not wanting to be seen to be keen railwaymen playing trains, had by the 1980s come to be the overriding ethos – thus nobody wanted to work on the railway. The railways were a basket case and only a basket case would want to work on them. This was a major fly in the ointment of the privatization agenda – how on earth can you persuade people to purchase something when that something is constantly held up to ridicule and contempt?

> When a company is in retreat, torn by arguments and ridiculed by the press, the morale of its workforce is soon eroded. This in turn affects attitudes to customers, and the downward spiral accelerates. The High Speed Train – in reality only a small part of the vast efforts made to improve British Rail – has re-awakened some of the old railway pride.
>
> (Whitelegg et al., *HSTs*, p. 180)

The HSTs may well have been the flagships, they might well have had some impact on the public image of the railway and there is every possibility that they helped to stem the tide of falling passenger numbers. However, this picture should be qualified. The reductions of journey times were the real revenue winners, and several factors combined to improve these journey times, including track and signalling as well as faster locomotives.

In 1968 the Ministry of Transport talked of railways offering 125 m.p.h. services by 1973, rising to 150 m.p.h. by 1978. As we have seen, top speeds had risen to 162 m.p.h. by 1979. However, the speed of service trains is still some way behind the top-speed record, and even the 225 k.p.h. services brought about by the introduction in 1989 of the Class 91 electrics to the East Coast metals have only brought maximum service speeds up to 125 m.p.h., which are possible only over a limited number of sections of even the East Coast main line.

The 1980s saw passenger services over the major trunk routes dressed up as Intercity – a concept borrowed from the old GWR. 'Designer' 125 trains, with their image of 'futuristic excitement', were to be the means by which the negative images would be dispelled and the railway's importance to national economic life restated. On the other side of the coin, however, the one-time stars of the East Coast main line, the Deltics, were being requested for rail tour work, just as the A4s and sundry other steam locomotive types had been as steam ended. The supercession of the initial diesel fleet (D201 first worked the 'Flying Scotsman' in 1958) by the HSTs came to be more than simply an improvement in motive power and rolling stock. It became part and parcel of a strategy designed to create a saleable product – not a railway journey, but a railway network.

Alongside the re-imaging of the railway journey were new divisions of the railway itself and, to complement these new means of accounting, new 'profit centres'. Unlike the 'old' railways which had to be 'subsidized', Intercity was to be a profitmaker. Gone were the 'Big Four', gone too were the old regions, replaced by networks, Intercity, Regional Railways, or Metro Train, as geography and commercial constraint dictated. Partnerships between railways and local authorities created the Metro operations, an initiative which saw the re-opening of some stations and the building of new ones to service the shifting urban population. This whole process also put pressure on the training and recruitment of footplate grades and culminated in the 1988 Traincrew Agreement:

> In 1988 the Traincrew Agreement was introduced. This changed radically Driver Training on British Rail, and the promotional arrangements were also altered, in that other staff on British Rail were given the opportunity to apply to join the Footplate line of promotion to become a Driver and subsequently no new entrants were set on in the role of Drivers for some time.
>
> (Tomlinson, Introduction, p. 12)

By 1991 the British Railways Board had published *Future Rail – the next Decade*. In this work one of the stated aims is the 'running of a safe, reliable and quality railway'. With this aim comes the recognition that this objective can only be achieved with the support of the staff:

> A structure of competence based qualifications of which driver training is an integral part is being put in place to secure the operation, to ensure the progress of talented men and women to positions of higher responsibility, and to support the quality initiatives taking place throughout the railway.
>
> (quoted in Tomlinson, Introduction, p. 14)

The extent of competence based qualifications has now extended to the point where men like driver Hobson, enginemen for thirty or more years, are now going to have to undertake NVQ certification, as have men like Mr Tomlinson, the Driver Training Manager, whose own railway career started in 1960 as an engine cleaner at Langwith Junction. Even the trainers are trained and nobody is anybody without a certificate.

As the 1980s drew to a close the major part of the footplate revolution was complete: new methods of training, new routes of promotion, a vastly different working environment, a changed landscape to that working environment, new rule books, new uniforms, the loss of regular mates, the ending of the eight-hour day and more had been accomplished. Pay, pensions and holidays, however, still lagged behind those of other European footplate workers. Retirement is still later, the level of pension is still less, holiday entitlements shorter, hourly rates lower and the working week longer – hardly a recipe for attracting and retaining the 'talented men and women' that would be required to deliver the 'safe, reliable, quality, railway'.

The final years of the decade also saw the introduction of new computer technology and electrical engineering combining to create a new generation of electric locomotives. In particular, Class 91 electrics were being built to operate the newly electrified East Coast main line, which was switched on as far as Leeds in time for a scheduled service to commence on 11 March 1989. This coincided with the installation of the first of the 'flashing' green signal systems on the Stoke–Warrington section of the East Coast main line; this was the first of the sections over which 'trial' 140 m.p.h. service speeds were to be made – though they are still not officially sanctioned.

In 1986 driver Hobson was again on the move – this time from Neville Hill to Gateshead – and again this move was essentially concerned with avoiding redundancy and improving the type of duty to be undertaken. Flying up and down the East Coast main line is, even without the steam locomotive, a more exciting prospect than going round and round the York–Leeds–Harrogate circle; because of the mileage bonus system it is also more highly paid.

Before leaving the 1980s there was a little incident in the introduction of the Class 91s which appears to have been a crafty marketing ploy. The High Speed Trains had been referred to not only as HSTs but also as 'Intercity 125 trains' – an indication of their maximum service speed, 125 m.p.h. When the new Class 91 services were brought into being they were referred to as the '225 trains', making it appear to the unthinking or the uninitiated that speed had risen by 100 m.p.h. The real difference in speed was 15 m.p.h., but the '140 train' does not have quite the same ring to it. However clean and bright the technological developments, and however slick and sophisticated the image changes, as the 1980s ended the railway's future and that of its employees was as uncertain as ever.

CHAPTER 5

All Electric

Back in the old days when steam ran everything, the romance of the railway was taken for granted: the tear in a lover's eye could be blamed on smoke smuts. But were those days really that romantic, or was the romance an attempt to hide the rather more stark realities? Carnforth station, scene of the 1949 movie *Brief Encounter*, is an unbelievably dreary place, dank and chill, its subways more likely to be the scene of a mugging than a romantic tryst. The tales of footplate life are not unlike this, talking up the good times even though they may have been 'rough' trips. The weeks spent cleaning clinker out fireboxes, shovelling char out of smokeboxes and raking out the ashpans are scarcely the stuff of legend – no 'Night Mail shovelling white steam over her shoulder' in this picture. Much of the romance of the steam era was based on events, circumstances and human interactions that have since disappeared – after all, there's no mate on driver-only or single-manned duties, no bad steamers to conquer, and the Class 91 electric on the East Coast main line will go up Stoke bank faster than *Mallard* went down it, and not a whiff of garlic except in the restaurant car.

The Introduction raised the question of romance and suggested that 'responsibilty' would be a far better choice of adjective to apply to the footplate profession. There is another word which is also applicable – continuity. Driver Hobson, though he does not drive a Stirling 8' single, nor one of Gresley's Pacifics, up and down the land is no less an engineman than the likes of drivers Sparshatt, Hoole or McKillop – the real difference is in the context in which he is viewed and the machinery with which he carries out his duties. The continuity is real in other aspects, which is seen through driver Hobson's own narrative.

Throughout our conversations what has concerned driver Hobson has been the men he has worked with, even though today a large proportion of his work is on his own. Of the things he has to say about these men foremost is their skill as enginemen and the valuable lessons they have taught him – in this respect his narrative is grounded in the skills and knowledge most commonly associated with the steam age enginemen. His story parallels that of those enginemen of old, and on those occasions when he is accompanied by a trainee driver Hobson enjoys nothing more than to pass on his knowledge of railway working. However, it should not, for one moment, be imagined that as a result he lives in the past; far from it:

Sure I'd love to be out there running the East Coast with steam: being an engineman was why I started this job. I've even toyed with the idea of paying for a place on Clive Groome's course, so I qualify as traction trained – but after the do with *Blue Peter* no one on East Coast wants anything to do with steam specials, but that doesn't stop you dreaming.

If they had to modernize, this is the railway we should have had. These 91s were built for the East Coast, they're the right tools for the job – this is the modernization we should have had thirty years ago. They should have worked out the steam engines instead of cutting them up, and then gone over to electric, cutting out the diesels altogether – most of them were no better than the steamers they replaced anyway. The class 91s are, undoubtedly, the best tackle I've had, and though you get the odd niggly problem the only serious do I've had was on the road between Edinburgh and Glasgow near Prestonpans. Ironic, really, because it was the pantograph that was the problem – it had been torn off. What a night that was, middle of winter, blowing a gale if not a hurricane (it was the wind that had caused the damage to the pantograph), and no power – I thought I was going to freeze to death. When I tried to get off the engine I was almost blown away. I was walking at about 45 degrees, I've never known a night like it. (Driver Hobson stands 6 ft 2 in and weighs about 14 stones.)

(driver Hobson, 1995)

What made the so-called 'ace' enginemen of the past was their knowledge of the road, of their engine and its capabilities, of their mate and his ability; but above all it was a confidence in their own judgement. In driver Hobson's case the only one of these to be lacking is the mate or, more specifically, the fireman, though on some of the present-day round-trip London workings – those involving running at 125 m.p.h. or more – he does have a second driver in the cab.

'Ace enginemen' are also characterized by their dedication to the job, and here again driver Hobson is the equal of his steam-age counterpart. He was awarded the Silver Swallow, which is East Coast's way of honouring staff who have acted beyond the call of duty. In driver Hobson's case this involved being stranded near Tuxford for six hours because a flash over had burned out a whole section of the overhead. Once power was restored not only did he work through to Kings Cross but he remained on duty and worked back a semi-fast to Newcastle to ensure that the hundreds of passengers who had been stranded at Kings Cross for six hours reached their destinations – albeit late. Award-winners receive a sterling silver swallow and are taken out for the day by the company. In driver Hobson's case this was a visit to Burleigh House near Stamford in Lincolnshire, hot air balloon rides and being wined and dined like a lord.

The East Coast's claim to be Britain's fastest railway is all well and good but running at high-speed, over long distances, places a continuous demand upon the driver to remain alert. Each driver has his own strategy to deal with this problem and what works for one may not do so for another:

You have to think ahead all the time. It still has something of the old steam days about it, like knowing where you can catch first glimpse of a signal, or knowing where the ones you don't see until the last minute are when you're running up to the limits, trying to make time. Knowing your breaking points is the important thing now. I had this chap in the cab just the other week, he was from the TUCC [Transport Users' Consultative Committee], and I could tell from his reactions that there were times he thought we weren't going to stop, he kept looking at the speedometer, at me and at the station, but knowing where and when to shut-off and start to brake is one of the ways to make a bit of time back today.

(driver Hobson, 1995)

Driver Hoole, the legendary East Coast speed merchant, and driver Hobson may drive (or have driven, in the case of the former) very different types of locomotive but they speak the same language, understand the same problems and use their knowledge of the road and their engine to solve them. One thing driver Hoole might have found difficulty with today is the use of radar speed traps, or radar speed checking via the use of hot-box detectors, though in the case of the latter once you have worked out where they are they no longer represent a problem.

There was a time when British Rail were advertising their wares by using the idea of being caught speeding – it doesn't happen on the train! Not to the passengers it doesn't, but to the driver it is another matter. In the 1950s and 60s, to publish details of high-speed running – those runs where line speed limits were broken – could have serious consequences for the driver, though as steam faced its final curtain there was a little relaxation and a turning of the proverbial blind eye. Even the staff sent out in the 1960s to catch the speeders took a fairly laissez-faire attitude to the proceedings – but not any more. The one concession, however, is that speed records taken from the Class 91's on-board computer are not admissable evidence of a particular driver speeding. But getting caught out by hot-box detectors is not the only way to be caught speeding: radar speed traps have come a long way since that first experiment back in 1968, and they are regularly set up at the faster stretches of the main line routes. Breaking the speed limit is still a serious disciplinary offence.

Because you have to think ahead all the time, it helps if you have some way of focussing on what is coming up. I try to drive through the route as though I was running with an A3 or 4, thinking about the gradients, where I can ease the power off, using the road to help control line speed. I could just set the target speed and leave it to the computer, but doing it the way I do helps the concentration and helps to stop boredom creeping in. Not everyone drives like this, though: some of the lads who've started since 1970 give you some odd looks sometimes. Another way I remember the road is to remember all the old boxes, but whatever way you do it the important thing is to know exactly where you are; if you are going to go for it you can only do so where you know exactly what is coming up. Things happen very, very fast when you're doing a mile in less than 30 seconds. Stopping nearly 500 tons of train at speeds in excess of 125 m.p.h. isn't like stopping a sports car.

(driver Hobson, 1995)

Not all the romance of the railway came from the contest between men, machines and the gradients; another important aspect was the routes and the scenery along them, the time of day and the season of the year. Here again there is much that has changed,

Driver Hobson in charge of No. 60019 Bittern *on an enthusiast special which took in Hull to Bridlington and Scarborough before returning to Leeds. This was just one of the many enthusiast specials worked by driver Hobson during his time at Neville Hill depot.*

but equally much that remains the same: glorious sunrises along the Northumberland coast, and views of the sun sinking behind the pines round Loch Cobbinshaw have not changed since the railways began. However, railways also run through the entrails of our major cities and these can hardly be described as romantic views, with their scenes of industrial wasteland and inner-city urban blight. Unlike the rural scenery, though, these visions do change, often removing familiar landmarks as they do so.

The advent of the Class 91s and the electrification of the East Coast route may have been long overdue when the London to York services saw their first electrics in September 1989, but now the electrification is completed there is no question about the improvements it has brought, not only in reduced journey times but also in the improvements to the footplatemen's working environment.

By September 1991 the whole East Coast route to Edinburgh was switched on and a high-speed special was run from Kings Cross to Edinburgh in a little under three and a half hours; regular service trains are not as fast as this, taking a little over four hours on average. The technology may all have been new, but the method of promotion was still the same tried and tested remedy that had begun with the railway age itself. Run a train as fast as you can from A to B, invite the media to come along for the ride, and then make the most of the ensuing publicity.

High-speed trains were not the only express service on the East Coast: the erection of the electric catenary was also carried out with alacrity, using skills and knowledge gained from previous electrification schemes and a specially constructed cable-slinging train. Driver Hobson played his part in the electrification, driving the Class 31 or 37 diesels used to haul the specially constructed trains:

> The trick was to keep a steady walking pace: the 31s were the best for this because you could just set them in notch 1. On the 37s you had to jiggle the controller a bit and maybe even rub the air brakes a little. The guys who did the stringing were like monkeys, I've had them on top of the engine at times when they've been going at it. During the week when the catenary itself was going up we worked the regular service trains right past men swinging about in the air alongside the running road – everything just kept going as normal.
>
> (driver Hobson, 1995)

Technology is not the only means by which change on the railways has been prosecuted: railway privatization is bringing big changes and more will almost certainly follow in its wake. By the late 1980s mass privatization was becoming a major priority of the Conservative government, and the railways were joining a growing list of state industries and public utilities being broken up and sold into private ownership. Ways and means were being devised to divide up the operation of the railway into a variety of saleable pieces, a process dubbed 're-commodification'. Over the years since nationalization numerous activities which had been built up by the former railway companies had been hived off: hotels, ferries and road transport were just some of the railway's other businesses which were transferred back into private ownership and sold off, in one instance for one pound, with of course the attendant loss of revenue to the railways themselves. And as the last decade of the twentieth century began it was the railways themselves that were to be returned to private ownership.

The road to privatization has seen the setting up of Railtrack; as its name suggests, it is a concept owing much to Amtrack in the United States, the Roscos (rolling stock operating companies) and the route franchises usually referred to by title (e.g. South West Trains) or by reference to the potential bidder (Branson Rail, Resurgence Railways, etc.) or some other such temporary appellation. One part of what remains of British Rail's freight businesses has had four different names in less than that number of years. As part of this process, driver Hobson and his fellow footplatemen in the service of Intercity East Coast no longer work for British Rail: their contracts are now held by Intercity East Coast, a Train Operating Company. Driver Hobson describes how it happened: 'We just got a letter one morning telling us that our contracts of employment were now held by Intercity East Coast.'

The train operating company hires the rolling stock from the Rosco and pays a fee to Railtrack to operate over their lines, stop at their stations and so on. They raise the money to pay for this from the fares they charge the passengers. The train operators contract out the maintenance of the rolling stock they hire and, providing all goes well and to plan, they should come out with a profit – having paid out for their train, their servicing and repair, for the tracks to run them on and the drivers to drive and conductors to conduct and restaurant car staff to cater.

Currently the East Coast train operating company is trying to persuade its workforce, drivers Woolf and Hobson included, to participate in a management buyout of the franchise and buy shares in the company. Why these men and women should wish to purchase shares in something without any obvious assets, other than possibly a seven-year franchise to run trains, is not entirely clear.

What was once a complete business, albeit one with a very hierarchical management structure, is now a mass of competing organizations with conflicting goals, different agenda, falling levels of co-operation and co-ordination and staffed by people who are rapidly becoming more concerned with whether or not they will still have a job next week than with the long-term future of the railway, or the needs of the passengers and customers they are supposedly trying to cater to.

Press reports constantly refer to problems of connections, particularly those where passengers are changing from one franchisee's route to another. The introduction of financial penalty clauses for late running is the driving force behind this particular difficulty, rather than a desire to have passengers miss a connecting service – though of course they inevitably do. This, however, is not the only area of railway operation affected by the privatization agenda:

> The current attitude of management is quite different from what we have been used to. Though I must say that a year or two back when my wife became ill I was accommodated by not having to do night shifts, which was very helpful, but I'm back in the thick of it today. The change has been in other ways: we've been invited to seminars, asked to participate in 'brainstorming sessions' on how we might improve our services to the passengers. They fed us, put us up overnight in a hotel. It was all very nice, but we don't even know if we'll have a job when this privatization thing is finished – will Richard Branson want his own staff? Will we have to apply for our jobs back, with a different company, probably on worse terms and conditions to those we currently suffer? It shouldn't be like this after thirty-three years' service. It's all well and good them calling us by our first names: just when you think maybe they're trying to put matters right they ask you what you think about lodging turns – if they knew us and knew the job they wouldn't ask such questions.
>
> (driver Hobson, 1995)

Taking the staff out in the way driver Hobson describes may well help to generate team spirit and to keep morale up – it also encourages suggestions from the staff which have been estimated to be worth about a million pounds of savings per annum. The exercises may also be based more on the desire of the incumbent management to put together the best possible bid for the franchise to run train services on the East Coast. Whatever the motivation, one thing is certain, as far as the men are concerned: it is all very new. However, given past performances it may well take more than a seminar or two, dinner and a 'hail fellow well met' attitude to gain any real trust from the workforce.

Running the trains over the East Coast route, for Gateshead crews like drivers Hobson and Woolf, means covering the whole route. When working to London two drivers work the turn because of an agreement which requires two crewmen to be in the cab on services operating at a line speed of above 110 m.p.h. On the 'north road' from Newcastle to Edinburgh and Glasgow with a 110 m.p.h. line speed limit, duties are single-manned. Over the London road the crew work 'contract': this means three round trips, usually followed by a break of three or four days. On the Glasgow–Edinburgh route it is common to go five times there and back again in the week's work.

The north run is favoured by driver Hobson on the grounds that the road is more interesting and generally more scenic. On either route the constant accompaniment of the driver's safety device re-sets and the bell or hooter of the AWS remind you that this is a workplace and not an 'away day' outing. The driver's safety device (sometimes known as the deadman's handle) and the AWS help to ensure passenger safety and allow high speeds to be maintained even in fog, but they cannot be said to provide the most appealing background to an eight- to ten-hour shift in the cab. The cab itself is draught-free and comfortable seating is provided, but one rather surprising feature is that the windscreen glass feels soft to the touch – a vaguely gelatinous sensation. A trip through the engine compartment is most illuminating: the on-board computer with its little red lights, lots of grey painted boxes and some very thick wires. If things go wrong there are travelling mechanics who can be called upon by using the in-cab radio telephone. Four of these technical riding inspectors cover the whole East Coast route: Gordon Campbell at Newcastle, Roger Senior at Doncaster, Steve Slater in London and Keith Mack over the border in Edinburgh. Between them these men cover all the mobile trouble shooting on Intercity East Coast; they can even plug into the Class 91's on-board computer and drive the train from a keypad.

Crews do have a working knowledge of their engines and there are several things which can be done by them in an emergency, to isolate or even override a fault or problem, but they cannot begin to tamper with the locomotive in ways they might have once done with a steam engine; there are no sticking clacks to hit with the coal hammer! In the case of electric locomotives, specialized knowledge is required in fault finding and repair, and special tools and equipment are generally required to complete these tasks. Having said that, there was little that a footplate crew could achieve by way of out on the road repair on the steam engine, so perhaps the positions have not altered that much, over the years, in this respect.

The on-board computer of the Class 91 electric locomotive is down-loaded at regular service intervals to give information on what the train or locomotive was doing at any part of its journey. This is the footplate the 1990s engineman inhabits. The microchip technology also controls and regulates the power flow to the drive chain when the controller in the cab is opened and is an integral part of the anti-slip mechanisms. One of the first bugs to be detected in this system was that the Doppler effect radar sensors which fed the information about wheel slip to the computer were fooled by standing water – the sensors tell the computer the wheels are slipping and the computer adjusts power to the traction motor – thus the train could be brought to a stand by the continued reduction of power to the traction motors. These motors are underslung and drive the bogie through a propshaft and universal joint not unlike that on a motor vehicle.

Unlike the early types of electric locomotives and some diesels, the Class 91s do

Driver Woolf at the controls. Behind him can be seen the control levers of the auxiliary driving position – used in shunting manoeuvres, as the side cab windows do not open. From this panel the driver can operate the train brakes and power up to around 10 to 15 m.p.h., looking out through the door to watch for shunt signals.

not have to be accelerated or decelerated notch by notch: the controller can be pulled fully open and the computer controls the levels of power transmission. The advantage of this system is that it has the effect of making recovery after neutral sections and shutting off before them a shorter sequence of events. As a result power is kept on longer and re-applied sooner – leading to higher averages point to point. In the new railway of the 1990s passing times and the 'booked' timings of the 'working timetable' are becoming of crucial importance.

(For anyone unfamilar with railway working the 'working timetable' is not the same document as the passenger timetable, though of course there are certain timings common to both. The working timetable contains not only intermediate timings between individual stations, but also such details as which road a particular train may be routed to run over, i.e. up main, up relief, up goods, in addition to other pertinent information about a particular route, the lengths of passing loops or other such features.)

Delay means money. If a train is late at a timed passing point, either Railtrack pays the train operating company or the train operating company pays Railtrack, depending on which of the bodies is deemed to be the responsible party for the lost time. This arrangement also applies to freight traffic, a situation which can lead to freight trains being run ahead of passenger services in order to avoid delay to the on-time freight by holding it for a late-running passenger service. It is not that this did not happen in the old days – it is that today there is no room for discretion, which was frequently used by signalmen to help the passenger service regain lost time. Today the chances are that the losses would be too great, essentially because of the financial penalties and benefits which now form an essential part of the operating environment.

> When you're pulling away from Motherwell, if you've had to stop, up towards Law Junction, there's a neutral section which you hit at under forty and because of the adverse gradient your speed drops as you go through it. This section is hard to time anyway; if there are any problems it is quite easy to pass Law Junction down. I had a run a week or two back and we had one of the traction motors isolated. I got a ticket for two minutes late passing Law Junction and there is nothing you, me or anyone else could have done to make the train go faster. Overall the 91s will time the train station to station even with a motor isolated, but some of the intermediate timings are so tight that you can easily be two minutes adrift and that's about £90 someone owes to Railtrack.
>
> (driver Hobson, 1995)

Class 91s are not the only locomotives in service on the East Coast route and both Class 90 electrics and the HSTs are, or have been, involved in running the services. The HSTs which had been introduced on the East Coast route in the late 1970s were by 1992 being taken out of service for refurbishment. At the same time certain members of the Class 90 electrics were given clearance for 125 running, upgraded from 110 m.p.h. This upgrade made them the ideal 'Thunderbird' if anything untoward happened to the Class 91s. The HSTs are of course still an essential part of the services offered by East Coast and at one time provided Gateshead crew with their longest turn of duty, working round to Middlesborough and then to Kings Cross, returning with a semi-fast. This service no longer runs, and passengers for Middlesborough no longer enjoy a through service to Kings Cross.

There are thirty-one Class 91s to cover twenty-six diagrams (i.e. a set series of services over a set time interval); this leaves five sets of which at least one is assumed to be under major repair and the other four undergoing the varying degrees of servicing demanded by the maintenance schedule. This is a tight ship. It has been subjected to cost cutting in recent months, and now, instead of hiring a Class 90 there are no stand-by electric locomotives, only the Class 47 diesels.

> There are turns of duty we call 'Thunderbirds' – because we sit around all day waiting for a breakdown and then when things go wrong we go 'to the rescue'. We used to have four Class 90 electrics as stand-by for the 91s but somebody decided that this was too costly, so now there is no back up if a Class 91 fails: it will mean cancelling the train. The problem with this arrangement was that if the 91 failed the Class 90 wouldn't time the train over the London road: even flat out you were losing time in all the 125 m.p.h. sections.

For breakdowns *en route* or power failures we have a Class 47 diesel; funny thing is they've even named one of them 'Thunderbird'. What is happening here is another possible problem. If we work a loco-hauled train, we should have worked in this way with a train during the previous six months. If we haven't then according to the latest health and safety we shouldn't work the job. You could be booked 'Thunderbirds' and not have been on a loco-hauled train and if there was a failure you could refuse to go because of the new rulings.

Another of the changes in recent months has been that we just go for it all the time, never mind being early. If we have to wait fifteen minutes outside Kings Cross, or wherever, that's not our problem: we're not late and that's all that counts. What is going on is just silly, everyone is looking to pass the blame. Every day we still have to fill out the driver's ticket: this hasn't changed since I started, it's still exactly the same as it was in 1960. Now, though, if anything has happened or there has been any delay there are forms to fill in for any signalling irregularity, forms to answer if we pass a timing point late, there's a form for everything. You get more paper work today than ever there was in steam days. You can spend half an hour at the end of your shift just scribbling on bits of paper.

(driver Hobson, 1995)

On the journey I made with driver Hobson, on board Class 91 No. 91011 *Terence Cuneo*, there was a signalling irregularity – what had been a one-yellow signal went back to red as our train approached and as a result the first three vehicles passed the signal at danger. After donning his high-vis vest driver Hobson descended from the cab and set off to telephone the signalman. We were ordered to proceed at caution, and the signal change was blamed on a problem with the point interlock. When we returned to Newcastle driver Hobson had to complete a form documenting the nature of the incident, the number of the signal and the instructions he was given. In theory he should have had an explanatory reply slip within fourteen days – two months after the event driver Hobson was still waiting. By contrast, within forty-eight hours of the delayed passing at the Law Junction timing point, driver Hobson was given a form asking him to explain why he was late. The isolated traction motor was accepted as a sufficient answer – but who pays? The simple answer is Intercity East Coast as they are responsible for maintenance and it is a maintenance fault. The less simple answer is everyone pays, taxpayer, passenger, footplateman: all lose in some way or another from the present round of railway interference.

The shifting of accountability in what is taking place in the run up to the sale is one of the more insidious aspects of the whole privatization business. To add to the claims of more choice, perhaps there should be the caveat 'less accountability'.

Running trains on the East Coast route for the men of what was once the famous Gateshead shed means, for the most part, booking on duty at Newcastle Central Station. Drivers book on and off at a sliding glass window let into the wall of a ground-floor room – the domain of the roster clerk and duty foreman. From here driver Hobson receives daily notices or any special instructions. On the day of my visit hanging alongside the window was a list of names of sponsors for a driver who was to run for charity in the Great North Run (the 1990s manifestation of public duty?). In another ground-floor room were the notice boards which contained details of the duties of the four links, A–D, along with p-way and other formal notices. The locker room, toilets and washroom as well as the common mess room were up several flights of stairs deep in the labyrinth of passages above the station buffet and bookstall. It has to be said that the mess room lacked atmosphere of any kind, the only occupant on my visit being a porter eating sandwiches for his lunch.

Working the Class 91s does seem to give the men involved a certain cachet. Whether it is comparable with that of the men who worked the line with Gresley's Pacifics, that I cannot say, but what is unarguable is that drivers Woolf and Hobson exhibit the same degree of confidence, the same level of responsibility and commitment as those enginemen of old were reputed to possess, and they see themselves as being fairly representative examples of their fellow enginemen, modest of their achievements, ready to acknowledge the ability of others to be able to do what they did when running the 154 m.p.h. record breaker. The traction may have changed, the social life and the level of sophistication may have altered almost beyond recognition, yet there is still a remarkable degree of similarity between the characters of today's footplatemen

The speedometer reads 125 m.p.h. as we look over driver Hobson's shoulder. The white sheet on the right is the timing sheet; above it is the radio telephone. To the left of the speedometer is the target speed selector and below it is a row of fault lights.

and the heroes of the age of 'corridor tenders' – responsibility and continuity, it would seem, are inseparable from railway footplate work.

As we have seen, railway footplate experiences can and do vary widely depending on the depot and the work it covers; this is as true today as it was in steam days. Life for the footplatemen working on the East Coast route still involves shifts, starting and finishing at all hours of the day and night. Though the P and D turn no longer involves raking out ashpans and crawling under the engine in between the motion to oil the middle big end, it does still exist, and driver Hobson, despite his thirty-three years on the job, still takes his turn at getting stock ready.

Clocking on at midnight at Heaton depot, the home for the Class 91s of driver Hobson's section of the railway, the footplateman whose turn it is to cover the P and D job will spend his night shunting and checking the stock for the next day's services. Brake tests, pantograph checks, headlamp and tail lamp exams all have to be made. Though it may not sound much, there is a great deal of walking up and down, clambering in and out of the cabs at either end of the train.

In addition to being checked and examined, the stock is washed, service water tanks filled, windscreen washers and wipers given the once over. This is not a job to relish on a cold winter's night on Tyneside, but it is part of the routine of top link drivers and provides a sobering counterpoint to the image of the dashing engineman in his 140 m.p.h. express, and hardly seems to square at all with brainstorming seminars and bed and board in a comfortable hotel.

When each train has been checked and prepared it receives a 'poise' sheet. This certifies that all the various checks have been made and details any defects or problems, such as the isolation of a traction motor or out of service toilets. The poise sheet has become an essential document and the lack of one constitutes grounds for not moving the train until one has been produced or the checks have been carried out to the driver's satisfaction.

Changed atmospheres in the realm of safety and the alterations to the footplate crew training programme have brought changes to the duty roster. Drivers are now booked to have safety training days at approximately six-weekly intervals in addition to the regular bi-annual checks on the rules and regulations; their purpose is to keep crews aware of changes in safety regulations. The introduction of new technology also brings with it new training requirements; the introduction of the cab radio resulted in all the drivers undergoing a two-day training programme in much the same way as if they were learning new types of traction.

While this new emphasis on staff training and safety is to be applauded, there is, perhaps, more than a touch of cynicism involved. One of the biggest stumbling blocks to the privatization process is in the area of safety: it is this area which causes the would-be insurers of any privatized railway network the biggest nightmares, and its cost could be an important factor in determining levels of profitability for any future owners of the railway's assets. Whilst such measures undoubtedly make life safer for passengers and crews alike it is somehow wrong for these things to be happening to satisfy commercial criteria rather than to fulfil any responsibility towards the workforce.

In terms of reduced journey times and increased frequency of services from some stations there certainly has been progress in running trains on the Intercity East

Coast. If, however, greater comfort and luxury are to be part of the yardstick then things look less rosy. There is today an atmosphere of cost cutting which goes beyond what is necessary, and there are instances where the effects have been to reduce comfort and thus pleasure in the journey. Though from a footplate perspective the cab of the Class 91 is a quieter, cleaner place than that of the cab of an A4, it does lack that little frisson that comes with any long-distance steam working.

The modern day East Coast engine driver unmistakably inhabits a different world from that of his steam age counterpart, but there can be little doubt that there are those enginemen on the East Coast today who in their own terms are every bit as dedicated and skilled in their work as any of those men eulogized in countless tales from the footplate written during the age of steam.

CHAPTER 6

154 m.p.h. and No Garlic

Running a 154 m.p.h. record-breaking train was not an idle whim dreamed up in some railway adman's lunch break: it was brought about by the activities of Peterborough City Council in its promotion of 150 Years of Railways in Peterborough – though of course the railway concerned was not the East Coast main line, nor even its distant predecessor the Great Northern Railway. Indeed, Peterborough's first railway was courtesy of George Hudson, the arch-enemy of the old GNR and its direct route to the North.

The first line into Peterborough was from a connection to the London and Birmingham which, through amalgamation in 1846, became a major constituent of the London North Western Railway. This line branched from the LNWR at Blisworth and was part of Hudson's and the Euston Confederacy's spoiling tactics to prevent the GNR ever going anywhere. The line was built while the promoters of the London & York (the original title for the Great Northern Railway) were still trying to get their Bill through Parliament in 1845 at the very height of Railway Mania. Though the initial idea to hold the celebrations in 1995 belonged to Peterborough, Railtrack and the train operator Intercity East Coast both wanted to be party to the event and, as two influential boardroom figures from these concerns lived in the Huntingdon area and were equally keen to see some sort of record attempt, the scene was set.

The real shame about choosing to commemorate these particular events is that 1995 was also the centenary of the much more famous 'Railway Races to the North', which took place between July and August 1895. This would have been a much more significant event to celebrate, particularly as they did succeed in lowering the journey times to Scotland by substantial amounts. Perhaps more important, they actually concerned the East and West Coast routes to Scotland rather than a railway backwater such as the Hudson route to Peterborough. Unfortunately one has to acknowledge that few have heard of the Northampton & Peterborough Railway and that fewer still are likely to travel to Peterborough from Euston via Wellingborough. In all likelihood Peterborough would never have developed as an engineering centre and commuter dormitory if its only railway link to the capital had been the Hudson-owned route they chose to celebrate.

Having decided, however, upon celebrating 150 years of railway history in Peterborough, running a high-speed train at more than 150 m.p.h. is at least in keeping with an event celebrating railways, and Railtrack and Intercity East Coast appear to have done their best to ensure that not only did the event run smoothly but that maximum publicity was gained from the event.

Before the actual record-breaking event of 2 June 1995 there were two planned test runs. After the first of these, the train set was not only examined but all the tyres were reprofiled in order to limit track damage. Reprofiling also alters the way the train responds on canted sections of track, but perhaps more important in events such as these, it ensures a smooth ride for all the media corps, as well as city councillors and celebrities, including Dr Mawhinney, who was not only Transport Secretary but also MP for Peterborough. Meanwhile, back in the cab an additional speedometer or data logger was installed as the standard ones fitted to the DVT do not register speeds as high as 154 m.p.h. The door locks too came in for special attention, problems having been experienced with the micro-processors which operate the mechanisms for the integrity of the 'door closed' safety system.

The two runs may best be described as a trial followed by a dress rehearsal. It would have been highly inappropriate if things had gone wrong on the day. 'The test runs helped us to work out the timings and where we could really have a go – Stoke Bank isn't the only fast piece of railway on the East Coast. It helped with

Stirling's 8' Single No. 1 and Gresley's Pacific No. 4498 Sir Nigel Gresley *represent over half a century of East Coast main line locomotive development. No. 1 was built in 1870 and the A4s began to see service in 1935. They are pictured together at the Shildon Cavalcade.*

the different braking performance resulting from the train being shorter and therefore lighter than a standard set' (driver Hobson, 1995).

Organizing an event of this importance is not an overnight task. Six weeks earlier the first test train was run at 152 m.p.h. and taken out of service for the wheel profiling to be carried out and other technical modifications made. (The overall project co-ordinator was Robin Lumb; Steve Buxton, of Interfleet at Derby, dealt with the technical side.)

Important though the technical aspects may be, with a train load of VIPs and journalists just waiting for the tiniest slip, the Public Affairs department was every bit as vital. Co-ordinating this aspect of the event was David Potter for Railtrack, with the major part of the exercise being conducted by East Coast Public Affairs from their headquarters in York. Heading this team was Jeff Nichols, supported by Sue Wells and David Mallendar. This was their biggest event in ten years and more than sixty journalists applied to travel in the train on the day. Coverage of the run was given in more than fifteen national television news broadcasts, beginning with coverage live from Newcastle station as the historic departure took place and going on throughout the day until News at Ten on ITV. Further coverage was given on Sky TV, regional television news and on the radio; again both national and regional stations were involved. More than seventy separate articles appeared in the national and local press, including a front-page story in the *Guardian* and a leader column in the *Times*.

Just fifteen minutes before departure time as No. 91031 Sir Henry Royce *and train roll into Newcastle to collect their passengers for the record-setting run. (photograph © C.J. Marsden)*

Driver Hobson, however, was not enamoured of the press coverage:

> One of the things that bugged me about the press, both the television and the papers, was that they seemed to want to knock what we had done, how the French went faster every day of the week, that sort of thing. In one of the TV interviews I was saying how we had set our record over a railway that was built by Stephenson in Victoria's reign and that the French and the Japanese ran their high-speed trains over specially constructed routes, with locomotives nearly three times more powerful than ours, but they cut those bits out – they didn't seem to be able to enjoy what we had done, they were just looking for ways to put the record down.

(driver Hobson, 1995)

In general terms the press concentrated on the record speed and, as driver Hobson commented, they tended to do so with their own agenda. Driver Hobson sees the record pragmatically: in Britain the best locomotive was achieving its record on the best railway driven by a top link crew. A more political agenda is apparent in the statement from Railtrack and East Coast, in which East Coast's managing director Brian Burdsall and his Railtrack counterpart Bob Clarke proclaim the event as 'a marvellous example of the ability of the new railway

Having attained 154 m.p.h. down Stoke bank, Class 91 No. 91031 Sir Henry Royce *approaches Peterborough on 2 June 1995, with Mk 4 DVT No. 82231 leading the special five-coach rake. (photograph © Brian Morrison)*

businesses to work together, forging better relationships for a succesful future'. What is important to Burdsall and Clarke is their ability to cooperate to generate the record, though the issue of the cooperative effort was largely ignored by the media. By contrast, in Dr Mawhinney's sound bite the record speed was cited as evidence of 'Britain's technological superiority'.

The tabloid newspapers went out looking for the 'man in the street' verdicts. Typical of the genre was this one from the now defunct *Today* newspaper: 'Francesca Sutton, 26, said: "If this train gets in the record books, that's all very well. But I'd be happier if they concentrated on getting me to work on time. They appear more concerned with publicity than passengers"' (*Today*, 3 June 1995). The *Daily Express* columnist Harry Cook spells out what he sees as the main function of the high-speed run: 'Yesterday's run on the East Coast main line between Darlington and Peterborough was seen more as a boost for impending rail privatisation' (*Daily Express*, 3 June 1995).

Inevitably, the tabloids could not refrain from dragging in their favourite topic, sex. Harry Cook's article ends with the comment, 'It comes just months after South Central was attacked for offering "dirty weekend" breaks to Brighton.' (Incidentally, the standard of accuracy of the tabloid reports left much to be

John Welsby, BR chairman, and Dr Mawhinney, Transport Secretary, facing the press on the platform at Peterborough after the record run. (photograph © C.J. Marsden)

desired. One misnamed the record-breaking locomotive *Sir Henry Royce* as 'engine Harry Royston' (*Daily Mirror*, 3 June 1995). Was this new down-to-earth image more in keeping with the paper's readership profiles?)

Thus there were many different agendas in evidence. Unfortunately the most important among them were not railway agendas but purely political ones, which reflects the extent to which railways have been politicized in Britain. Successive Conservative governments have attempted to discredit nationalized industry, although the true picture was always rather different: 'Early in 1980 a survey conducted by the *Economist* found that only two out of eighteen state companies were currently in the red' (Bagwell, *End of the Line*, p. 35). Indeed, state ownership versus private ownership of the railways has been a part of the agenda since railways began (Gladstone's Railways Bill of 1844 contained clauses which can be interpreted as a form of railway nationalization), and it has cost the railways dear. The high cost of Britain's railways was not all due to 'over engineering', much of it was due to Parliamentary interference and procedures. The constant friction over the issue of ownership of the railways has not only cost shareholders in the old railway companies a lot of money: it has also cost the taxpayer of today a great deal and is still doing so.

Everyone loses out. Drivers Hobson and Woolf have their efforts undermined and belittled by those grinding their axes on BR; the fare-paying newspaper readers lose out because they are being misinformed and overcharged; the taxpayer loses out because the money that should have been spent on improving the railways has been spent instead on merchant bankers, privatization consultants and ministerial advisors, as well as countless other expenses purely related to questions of ownership. Rather than Dr Mawhinney's 'technological superiority', itself a piece of political point-scoring, bogus claims thus add only to the misinformation surrounding the current railway debate.

The footplate crew are, of course, simply pawns in this particular game. From their own perspective they have enjoyed their fifteen minutes of fame – though even this has not been without its little problems: 'I've had three pieces of hate mail sent to me over the record run. They were not very nice: it's sad really that people get so jealous and upset over it all. What with the letters and the knocking, it sort of takes the edge off it a bit' (driver Hobson, 1995).

As for the run itself, let driver Hobson describe it in his own words:

I did the first half out of Newcastle. It was all set up for the publicity that the 154 record would be on Stoke Bank, but we were doing between 150 and 154 for about 11 miles between Darlington and York – down through Sessay and on to Beningborough. I was talking to the chap who'd been official time-keeper, Peter Semmens: he told me that he couldn't believe how fast we'd travelled over the Darlington to York section and had checked his figures several times to ensure he'd not made a mistake. We could have gone faster, but you have to stick to what has been planned, especially when there's so many people watching every move you make.

I knew we could easily make the speed because on the test run the day before we were stopped and yet still managed to top 150 before we reached

Beningborough. 160 m.p.h. would have been possible, maybe more: the decision to limit the speed to 154 m.p.h. had been taken higher up. Going ten or twenty miles an hour faster when you are already going at 150 m.p.h. is barely noticeable. Sitting in the DVT at 150 plus miles an hour is smoother and quieter than the footplate of a steam locomotive at 50 m.p.h. There is the constant resetting of the DSD pedal and the AWS bells to contend with, but the concentration is the main thing, that hasn't changed: you still have to keep a sharp look out at all times. There is a thrill, but it comes in different ways: it can't really be compared with a steam record, there's no sensation of the effort, no chimney chatter – it's almost an anti-climax on the leccy.

(driver Hobson, 1995)

Peter Semmens' column in *Railway Magazine*, 'Locomotive Practice and Performance', carried the full details of the run, from which the following information has been extracted. After the stop at Darlington speed rose to 125 m.p.h. at Eryholme, 142 m.p.h. at Otterington, 146 m.p.h. through Thirsk, 151 m.p.h. at Sessay and 153 m.p.h. at Pilmoor. From milepost 14 to Beningborough 154 m.p.h. was maintained over a distance of 8.6 miles. The start to stop time over the Darlington–York section was 22 minutes and 30 seconds, an average speed of 117.6

Facing the camera, drivers Hobson and Woolf stand alongside their train at Peterborough at the end of the record-breaking run. (photograph © C.J. Marsden)

m.p.h., with the Pilmoor–Beningborough pass to pass average being 153 m.p.h. This was actually a more impressive piece of running than the 154 m.p.h. on Stoke Bank, which was only over a short stretch and really done for the benefit of the press pack.

Both drivers will tell you that any of their number could have done what they did. This may be true, but the fact that driver Hobson was asked to change rest days in order to be available to work the train does seem to imply that management wanted him for the turn; and if they wanted driver Hobson then equally they must have chosen driver Woolf too. The railway's personnel department uses modern methods of employee profiling where time-keeping, absenteeism, disciplinary records and the like are computerized and sophisticated – no longer are men chosen for special or particular duties solely on the basis of the foreman's (driver team manager) or footplate inspector's (traction inspector) knowledge or likes and dislikes, as they have been in the past.

Making the record run was part and parcel of a day's work. No special training or diet was needed, no multi-million pound sponsorship deals beckoned, but there were one or two nice keepsakes for the crew. Both driver Woolf and driver Hobson were given models of the locomotive and commemorative plaques, modelled on those placed on *Mallard*. Identical plaques have been fixed to the locomotive 91031 *Sir Henry Royce*. The drivers and the locomotive were presented with their plaques at a public ceremony in Newcastle in July 1995.

After years of running railways down the desire to privatize them created circumstances in which it became necessary to talk them up – though the sale of the rolling stock raised only £1.8 billion, which was certainly below initial expectations. These changes may seem academic as the trains still run and the timetable is still set by British Rail, but change has become an integral part of the railway landscape.

Harking back to tradition has been one theme of the privatization agenda. For example, this is Brian Burdsall:

When I came to East Coast in 1992 as Route Director, I knew two things. Firstly, I had joined one of the best passenger railway operations in Britain, if not the world. Secondly Intercity East Coast has a history and tradition behind it that most employees are aware of and seek to live up to.
(Foreword to Body, *British Rail Routes*, p. 6)

A rose-tinted view of the past is often used to divert attention from a future of cuts in services and the less than profitable disposal of national assets, not to mention the ever likely possibility that further redundancies would follow from the process. In the cabs of the rolling stock 'under new management' one of the footplatemen's major concerns is job security – a factor often cited as vital in creating the 'traditional' company loyalty amongst the employees. Now, in the privatization-riddled 1990s, it is part of the stresses of the job:

What bothers me is are we going to still have jobs? There's all this talk about the ending of wages and being paid on salary. They want to bring in the salary, single manning on the London jobs, new rosters, it could mean more redundancies. The way things are now a large part of our wages are from bonus

Driver Hobson being presented with the commemorative plaque marking the record 154 m.p.h. run of 2 June 1995. Presenting the plaque is East Coast Financial Affairs Director Mike Thamm. (photograph © P.W.B. Semmens)

payments, especially mileage – these payments would go if they bring in payment by salary and so would some of the overtime payments, though some additional pay might be made if we work extra Sundays. Being salaried would make our pensions better because they are based on our basic rates, but unless they make the salary something like £20,000 a year a lot of the top link drivers at the high mileage depots like Gateshead are going to lose out; only those on current basic rates with no mileage and no night jobs will be better off all round.

(driver Hobson, 1995)

There are other ways in which the management's current claims to tradition are somewhat spurious. As we have seen, the public service tradition has been under attack: this was one of the very aspects of footplate life which, according to theory, engendered company or railway loyalty – what some have called a 'railway army ethos'. Respondents to Groome's survey remark that new entrants to the railway service 'see no tradition', are not 'initiated' into one and so are unlikely to create one, especially in circumstances in which companies change names, styles and ownership almost overnight.

Demographic trends add their own dimension to this problem: in 1992, some 70 per cent of British Railway's drivers were due for retirement by the year 2000. Most of these men are ex-steam footplatemen, and when they go any pretences to footplate traditions will vanish with them. A strong and thriving culture of 80,000 men has been reduced to 14,000, and even this number is set to fall, possibly to as low as 10,000 or 11,000. Attitudes of self help and self-sacrifice, also part of the tradition, have been undermined through the changes in working and training practices brought about by the ending of steam traction. Each of these losses on its own would be unlikely to make dramatic changes or disrupt the 'tradition', but when viewed collectively and alongside other changes in wider society the once distinct traditions of that footplate culture become diluted almost to the point of extinction.

One of the traditions that does seem to have a chance of survival is that of record setting and record breaking: this has been a part of the footplateman's job specification from the dawn of railways, and it is likely to continue. The fastest railed vehicle is an unmanned rocket-powered sled which hit 6,100 or more m.p.h., so there is plenty of room for improvement.

It is in the sphere of Continental journeys that the next stage of evolution in footplate work is taking place. The opening of the Channel Tunnel is creating new footplate opportunities as British crew begin to work trains to Paris and Brussels. As well as having to learn new roads and Continental methods of train working the crew on the Eurostar services are having to learn French, and part of this process involves them in going to France and living and working with French footplate crews – an echo of the 'in service' training of the steam age. Just as British crews are beginning to drive to the Continent, so the Continental drivers are beginning to work through to London.

The new horizons provided by the linking of Britain with Europe are not without their dark clouds, however. The divide and rule tactics employed in industrial disputes since the beginning of the industrial revolution are not solely confined to Britain. In December 1995 the French government was in severe difficulties with mass protest marches and strikes by public sector and transport workers over planned cuts in the French welfare state. During this dispute the French attempted to maintain the Eurostar services between Paris and Britain by utilizing British footplatemen, who of course were not party to the French protests. French trade unionists accepted the difficulties ASLEF members faced in being obliged to attempt to work normally while the remainder of the services were cancelled and pickets held up proceedings at the French side of the Channel Tunnel.

The expansion of the pan-European transport network is one of the most interesting developments from the perspective of opening new possibilities for footplate crews, both here in Britain and abroad. However, the present uncertainties, created by the dogma of privatization policy, can only be described as having an adverse effect on the lives and morale of the footplatemen. Few, if any, other bodies of public workers have coped with such dramatic decreases in their numbers alongside such fundamental changes in traditional craft skills, technological developments and loss of social standing. For a job and a tradition with such a large number of publications lionizing the men who upheld the traditions and who put the job first there have been precious few works lamenting the losses and the decades of decline.

The footplate revolution of the past thirty years has brought a vast change in the working environment and conditions of footplatemen's lives. Technological change is largely responsible for the former and social and political change the latter, but what does seem certain is that the revolution is not yet over: more far-reaching developments have yet to come.

One thing has not changed, however: footplatemen are still undervalued as their desire to get on and do the job leaves them open to exploitation. Despite all the changes, the divisions and the loss of some of the old traditions, strike action in 1995 won almost 100 per cent solidarity from ASLEF members, even though the ballot for strike action was won by only a small majority of members. How long they would have remained solid was not tested, but this is less important than that those who voted against came out in support of the majority, despite the very different arrangements that are beginning to appear in contracts of employment for footplate crew in different sectors of the railway.

Rail Express Systems drivers are on different contracts to those of Intercity East Coast or Regional Railways, with drivers on the Eurostar services on yet another style of contract. Eurostar drivers are paid on a knowledge basis and by a share in profitability, and knowledge of a form of traction or a language bring in extra cash. Divisions such as these do little to improve the pay bargaining situation of the footplatemen and, given past practice, look almost certain to be used in any future negotiations over pay and conditions; the divide and rule game is as unchanging as ever.

If the first footplatemen were those who operated Trevithick's first crude attempts at locomotion then 1996 is the 192nd anniversary of the craft of footplateman. Even if one were to take the Middleton Railway's successful use of steam traction in Leeds as being the first commercial basis for the existence of such a trade, then 1996 is the 184th anniversary. Either way this is a very long-lasting form of occupation. Throughout this time the footplatemen were respected and valuable members of the community; they were among the first sections of the working class to receive an education and they took great pride in fulfilling their public duties. As the twentieth century comes to an end it is far less possible to make such statements now.

The dwindling numbers, the decline in the perceived value to the national economy of the railways, loss of social status and a concomitant reduction in pay have all combined to diminish the footplatemen's position in society. The ending of the theatre of the footplate, the disappearance of the young acolytes at the end of every platform with their 'Can we cab it, Mister?', have also played their part, but despite these losses, drivers like Jimmy Woolf and Walter Hobson do uphold the long-held traditions of their craft. For all the propaganda, axe grinding and worse that the railways have suffered over the last thirty years and more. It still matters to these men that the trains run on time, and their responsibilities to their passengers remains paramount: the safe, quality, reliable, railway is *not* a British Rail mission statement – it is the ethos which the footplatemen have nurtured for almost two centuries.

Bibliography

Aldcroft, D.H. *British Transport Since 1914: An Economic History*, Newton Abbot, David & Charles, 1950

Bagwell, P.S. 'Early Attempts at National Organisation of the Railwaymen, 1865–1867', *Journal of Transport History*, 3, 2 (1957), 94–102

—— *End of the Line: The Fate of British Railways Under Thatcher*, London, Verso, 1984

—— *The Railwaymen: A History of the N.U.R.*, London, Allen & Unwin, 1963

Body, G. *British Rail Routes Past and Present: The East Coast Mainline, Kings Cross to Newcastle*, Peterborough, Silver Link Publishing, 1995

Bonavia, M. *British Rail: The First 25 Years*, Newton Abbot, David & Charles, 1981

—— *The Birth of British Rail*, London, Allen & Unwin, 1979

—— *The Organisation of British Railways*, London, Ian Allan, 1971

—— *Railway Policy Between the Wars*, Manchester, Manchester University Press, 1981

British Rail. *Rules for Observance by Employees*, 1950, with Amendments to 1961, London, Railway Clearing House, 1962

Ford, R. Obituary of G.F. Allen, *Guardian*, 17 August 1995

Groome, C. *Decline and Fall of the Engine Driver*, London, Groome, 1986

Hurcomb, C. *The Organisation of British Transport*, London, British Transport Commission, 1948

Kenny, R. *Men and Rails*, London, T. Fisher Unwin, 1913

Kingsford, P.W. 'Labour Relations on the Railways 1835–1875', *Journal of Transport History*, 1, 2, (1953)

—— *Victorian Railwaymen: The Emergence and Growth of Railway Labour 1830–1870*, London, Frank Cass & Co., 1970

McKenna, F. *The Railway Workers 1840–1970*, London, Faber & Faber, 1980

McKillop, N. *Ace Enginemen*, London, Thomas Nelson, 1963

—— *How I Became an Engine Driver*, London, Thomas Nelson, 1953

—— *The Lighted Flame: A History of ASLEF*, London, Thomas Nelson, 1950

Miller, T.C.B. Foreword to R.M. Tufnell, *The Diesel Impact on British Rail*, Bury St Edmunds, Mechanical Engineering Publications, 1979

Nock, O.S. *The Railway Engineers*, London, Batsford, 1955

Revill, G. *Trained for Life: Personal Identity and the Meaning of Work in the Nineteenth-century Railway Industry*, New Words, New Worlds: Papers and Proceedings: Reconceptualising Social and Cultural Geography, Lampeter, St David's University, 1991

Reynolds, M., *The Engine Drivers' Friend*, ed. M. Rickard, London, Hugh Evelyn, 1968

Simmons, J. Foreword to F. McKenna, *The Railway Workers 1840–1970*, London, Faber & Faber, 1980

Tomlinson, K. Introduction to *Route Learning/Simulation Training*, Trainee Drivers, Regional Railways North East, ref. 3180606A/2

Tufnell, R.M. *The Diesel Impact on British Rail*, Bury St Edmunds, Mechanical Engineering Publications, 1979

Wallis, P.R. *Men of the Footplate*, London, Ian Allan Publishing, 1954

Whitelegg, J. et al. (eds). *HSTs: Fast Tracks to the Future*, Hawes, Leading Edge, 1993

Young, R. *Timothy Hackworth and the Locomotive*, London, Locomotive Publishing Co., 1923

Index

Italic type denotes photographs